Vicki Lansky's

practical parenting

TRAVELING WITH YOUR ❀ BABY ❀

BANTAM BOOKS

TORONTO • NEW YORK • LONDON • SYDNEY • AUCKLAND

Editors: David Smith, Kathryn Ring, Toni Burbank, and Sandra L. Whelan

Special thanks to:
  Peggy Thomas, Pam Mueller, Colleen Finn,
  Mary McNamara, Peggy Markham, and Sherry Wood

Consultants:
  Carol Dingledy, Cosco/Peterson
  Neal Holton, M.D., International Travel Clinic,
    St. Paul-Ramsey Medical Center, St. Paul, MN
  Steve Frank, Minneapolis AAA Club
  Joy Sotolongo, American Academy of Pediatrics,
    Division of Public Education
  Dorothy Jordon, Travel with Your Children, New York City

Illustrator: Jack Lindstrom

Special thanks to the parents who shared their words and feelings. Their quotes are reprinted with permission from Vicki Lansky's *Practical Parenting* newsletter.

TRAVELING WITH YOUR BABY
A Bantam Book / July 1985

Library of Congress Cataloging in Publication Data

Lansky, Vicki.
  Traveling with your baby.

  (Vicki Lansky's Practical parenting)
  1. Infants—Care and hygiene. 2. Travel—Planning.
  I. Title. II. Series: Lansky, Vicki. Practical
parenting.
HQ774.L33 1985   613.6′8′0880542   84-91004
ISBN 0-553-34153-7 (pbk.)

  Published simultaneously in the United States and Canada

PRINTED IN THE UNITED STATES OF AMERICA

CW   0 9 8 7 6 5 4 3 2 1

Contents

Introduction

Yes! Take Them and Go

Travel with children is different from travel without them—no doubt about it. As you've discovered by now, they do change your life. And they will change the way you travel, but they don't have to prevent you from going out and about. The key to making your trip a good one for both you and your baby or toddler is careful planning, with your child uppermost in your mind.

Your own mental preparation is the first step. Your attitude will be the most important element of the trip. Learn to "expect the unexpected," and be prepared to change plans when a child becomes bored, overtired, or ill. And don't fantasize about reliving the "perfect trip" B.C. (Before Children). You can't, for example, just include a toddler in your spur-of-the-moment weekend jaunt or your tour of five Gothic cathedrals in one day.

If exploring new places to eat and sampling exotic foods have been important in B.C. trips, be prepared to de-emphasize the eating experience. However much you've enjoyed casual travel and taking "what the road offered," you'll find yourself making dinner reservations and phoning ahead. If you've loved moving from place to place as the inclination struck, you'll discover that children are more content when they're settled in at a home base and that constant packing and repacking with children is tedious. You'll want to slow down personally, too. Not only will your child be tired at the end of the day, you also will be more tired than you were on B.C. trips.

1

Planning Makes It Possible

What's the best time in a child's life, the best age, to begin to travel as a family? As in just about every other parenting decision, there are advantages and disadvantages to every stage and phase. Get out your favorite child development book, review all the things you can and can't expect from babies or toddlers your child's age, and apply them to the travel situations you'll experience.

Ages and Stages, Pros and Cons

Perhaps the most important thing to remember is that from infancy through toddlerhood, children don't really understand the concept of vacations. Every morning they wake to a new and exciting world; each day is different. They'll enjoy or not enjoy travel depending upon how they feel and what's going on at any given moment. Fatigue and hunger will be hardest on them—and therefore hardest on you.

Infants to 6 Months Old

A visit to relatives or friends (understanding ones!) may be your best bet for a first trip. Whatever you decide to do, try to keep it short and simple. The traveling life will be easiest for the nursing mother, who doesn't have to worry about bottles and formula and all the other accouterments of bottle-feeding. Still, if you'll be abroad and you're nursing, it is wise to take some ready-to-feed formula with you "just in case."

Infants usually can be counted on to sleep a great deal, and even poor sleepers are likely to doze off more easily because of the sound and motion of whatever mode of transportation you choose. And should you have a wakeful baby, at least it's more fun to be bleary-eyed away from home. The excitement of the trip may produce that extra burst of adrenaline that will help you through trying moments. On the other hand, if you have an infant suffering from colic, it would be wise to put off any travel until your baby has passed that three-month point when colic usually dissipates.

Packing, unpacking, and hauling around the extra amount of gear any baby needs may cause some tense moments. Still (especially if this is your first child), you and your spouse can both benefit from escaping the infant-dominated setting you've been living in.

Babies of 6 to 12 Months

When your baby is about 6 months old, you'll probably enter a time of major change, which some call the Rude Awakening. Your passive baby is no longer passive. He or she is now old enough to know who you are and when you're gone, but not yet old enough to be sure you're coming back. Exploration begins in earnest, and you'll soon discover that your baby's hand is often quicker than your eye. Your baby's developing mobility now makes it impossible to turn your back on him or her, and you can no longer plan to make an infant's sleeping "nest" out of any convenient spot.

Although attention spans are short, it's usually not hard to entertain a baby this age, especially if you don't mind repetition. (As one parent remarked, "If I never play 'Pat-a-Cake' or 'This Little Piggy' again, it will be too soon!")

On a relaxed vacation schedule, you may well have the pleasure of enjoying some of your baby's "firsts": crawling, walking, and—less thrilling—the emergence of new teeth.

Toddlers of 12 Months and Older

Toddlers' attention spans are slightly longer than those of babies, and you'll probably find that you can find a few extra moments for yourself while your child is occupied with a toy or a snack. You'll enjoy watching your child's reactions to and amazement at new sights and the growing ability to express wonder and delight in words (yes, and demands and complaints, too). "Delayed gratification" means nothing at this age, however; when a toddler wants something, he or she wants it *now*! Toddlers are self-centered, often seeming to feel that adults were put on earth only to gratify their wishes.

Structure, when possible, will be your best tool for this age child. Sticking as close as you can to bedtime routines, similar foods, and expectations from you can help smooth out tense times.

Toddlers require a lot of exercise, and you'll find frequent stops necessary if you're traveling by car. Your best trick will be sharpening your ability to anticipate your child's mood. If you can see hunger, frustration, boredom, or overtiredness coming, you can stop and do something about it before it gets out of control. After an exercise break, your toddler may resist being back in the car seat. You can make the transition easier by bringing out a new book or singing some good loud songs.

Grandma may be disappointed to find a child of 2 or so not as outgoing and loving as she might like. Strangers, even related ones, are welcomed by some children but not by others.

Vacations shouldn't produce battles or enforced discipline that really won't prove anything, and you should be able to enjoy your trip on your own terms. If others think you're spoiling your child (whatever *that* means), so be it.

And keep in mind that this is your vacation, too. You and

your spouse may need some time alone to help you deal with this intense family time. Don't feel guilty about going off alone—separately or together—on occasion.

Basic Planning

You can make your trip a wonderful adventure by using foresight and your best management skills. Keep your normal daily routines in mind as you plan for travel and for the days at your destination, allowing adequate time for rest and quiet as well as for active fun. Remember that you'll be living on CST—Children's Standard Time—and that a child's sense of time is different from yours. The uninterrupted six- or eight-hour drive that you find interesting and restful can be excruciating for a toddler, and the leisurely tours of gift shops you enjoy may turn into a "don't touch" sojourn of distasteful proportions for your child.

Your travel plans will most likely revolve around what you and your spouse think you'd enjoy with children along. Time, money, and family obligations tie into that decision.

- First, send for travel information offered in newspaper travel sections. At the very least your child will enjoy the photos with you and the chance to tear up the brochures later.

- Check into the availability of activities especially geared to young children. Travel guides usually list some, and you can write to local chambers of commerce for other ideas.

- Plan your outings with the children, rather than the adults, in mind. For example, you *know* that activities that will require standing in line for any length of time will not work for a child, no matter how terrific the attraction. The same goes for any extremely crowded or noisy places, and any strictly-for-adults entertainment. And seeing the

Grand Canyon will not be a memorable experience for a 2-year-old!

- Be aware that visits to museums and galleries will be covered quickly, not in your previously leisurely fashion, if your children are too old to be content to ride quietly in front- or backpacks. Your toddler may be more interested in the steps to a museum than in the exhibits; allow time for him or her to explore such preferred wonders.

Specialized Travel Services

Travel with Your Children (TWYCH)
80 Eighth Avenue
New York, NY 10011
(212) 206-0688

TWYCH is a resource information center that researches and provides detailed information that will make your family vacation a holiday for all. Contact TWYCH for prices for their newsletter and other publications (e.g., *Cruising with Children* and *Skiing with Children*). Family membership also available. This is not a travel agency.

Familyworld Tours
16000 Ventura Boulevard, Suite 200
Encino, CA 91436
(818) 990-6777

This travel agency offers planned, escorted, mainly international tours where you *must* have a child along to go. Trips are offered with children from ages 4 months and up. Include a long self-addressed, stamped envelope when sending for their trip planning kit and questionnaire.

Planning in Detail

- Make a list (or several lists) of everything you will need, including clothing, equipment, toys, and food. Decide where and how it will all be packed, and check off items you need to purchase as you get them. Shopping later for small, forgotten things can add unnecessary expense.

- Go a step further, if you wish, and prepare a "countdown" schedule, indicating the days certain duties should be performed, such as giving a key to the neighbor who will water the plants, taking a pet to the kennel, and doing the last load of laundry.

- Try to arrange the timing of your trip so you arrive at your destination fresh and rested, ready to begin the fun. Having time to explore new surroundings before bedtime often makes children less apprehensive about going to sleep.

- Take your infant's feeding schedule (if there is one) into consideration when planning a day's activities.

- Make a copy of your itinerary, if it's at all detailed, to leave with a grandparent, a neighbor, or another appropriate person.

- Assure a hassle-free homecoming by leaving an adequate supply of basic necessities at home—diapers, formula, baby food, a meal or two in the freezer—so you won't have to go to the store as soon as you arrive.

When our son was a year old, we went to California. We tried to compromise by doing the kid stuff in the morning and the adult stuff later in the day. Then if he slept through it, he didn't miss much.

Joan Grunberg, Chicago, IL

- Assign one adult to make the final check for closed windows, flushed toilets, disconnected appliances, and such.

Preparing the Family

Taking a weekend "practice run" is good preparation for an extended trip. You'll find the planning, packing, and traveling exercises will be helpful when you undertake the real thing, and you and your spouse will get an idea how things will work on the longer trip.

There is little you can do to prepare a baby for travel, other than keeping yourself organized and seeing that your baby is clean, fed, and rested before you set out. It is possible, though, to prepare a toddler for a trip.

Special for Toddlers

- Go to the library or a bookstore and get children's picture books that show your mode of travel.

- Use toys as props for your explanations. With a big map and a tiny car or airplane, show how you'll cover the distance "from here to way over there."

- Visit an airport or train depot, if you'll be using either of those modes of travel, so your child can become familiar with the noise and activity of departure and the sight of a real plane or train.

- Discuss time and distance with a child who's old enough to understand. Children's travel experiences often are limited to trips to the store, and the idea of days and nights away from home may be confusing.

- Talk about the people you'll see, if you'll be visiting friends or relatives. Get out the album and let your child see their pictures.

A Little Preventive Medicine

The last thing you need or want on a vacation is a child who doesn't feel well. Many problems can be prevented if you think ahead.

- Be wary of your child's contacts for two weeks or so before you leave. You don't want anyone to be exposed to even a cold, yourself included.

- Don't schedule vaccinations or immunizations just prior to your trip. Babies often have reactions that disturb their eating and sleeping—which you will not want to add to your list of concerns.

- Schedule medical checkups for the children before you go, if you suspect anything at all is not normal. Seeing a doctor is especially important if you'll be flying, since even a slight ear infection or a cold may cause a child severe ear pain when the cabin air pressure changes during takeoffs and landings.

- Consider carrying or buying bottled water for drinking and mixing with formula. Even good-quality drinking water can cause stomach upsets in small children, simply because it is *different* from what their system is used to.

- If you are switching to disposable diapers in anticipation of your trip, do so well in advance to see if there is a skin sensitivity to any specific brand.

One problem you may encounter is diarrhea, especially if you are traveling out of the country. But you don't have to travel far afield for it to occur. It can be caused by changes in drinking water, new or unusual foods, changes in routine, or simply the excitement of a trip. (See page 103 for more information on preventing and treating diarrhea.)

One last precaution you may wish to take, especially if you

have a costly trip planned, is trip cancellation insurance. This can usually be bought through travel agents and will cover lost costs if you are forced to cancel your trip. When you are figuring out how much you need to insure your trip, check into real and refundable expenses so you don't purchase more insurance than necessary.

Ounce-of-Prevention Checklist

- Your own first-aid kit, complete with Band-Aids, adhesive tape, sterilized pads, antiseptic cream, diaper rash ointment, any prescription medications and the prescriptions for them, rectal thermometer and petroleum jelly, a nasal aspirator for the flu season, syrup of ipecac (to induce vomiting in case of poisoning), baby acetaminophen (such as Tylenol) or baby aspirin, and a first-aid book.
- Insect repellent, sunscreen lotion (with PABA), etc., depending on your destination.
- Tweezers and needle for the inevitable splinter.
- The phone number of your pediatrician or family doctor.
- Your favorite baby-care book, if only to give you peace of mind.
- Your medical insurance card.
- Adult acetaminophen or aspirin for you. (Traveling with little ones has its trying moments.)

Reservations

If this is your first trip with your child and you'll be staying in a hotel or motel, you'll probably be more comfortable at a family-oriented establishment. Travel agents can be especially helpful here as will be state-by-state guidebooks from bookstores, libraries, or the AAA.

A fancy resort *may* work for you, as the rare, well-behaved child can be appreciated, but it will be important for you to accommodate yourself to the wishes of guests who really *do not want* children.

Accommodations

- Make motel, hotel, or resort reservations as far ahead as possible, especially if you're traveling at popular vacation times.

- Keep in mind that a motel on the outskirts of a town is more apt to offer play space and playground equipment than a downtown one.

- Check your reservations; be sure any necessary deposits have been made and that rooms will be held for your arrival. Then take those vouchers with you.

- Always ask about accommodations, amenities (especially swimming pool facilities and hours), and prices with children along. Many of the major chains offer special family rates, and most provide cribs free or at nominal fees. Some supply small refrigerators and/or laundry facilities.

Best Rooms to Request with Children

- Ask for a ground-level room in a motel to save yourself the trouble of hauling little ones and luggage up and down stairs.

Hotel/Motel Chains

	Toll-Free Reservations	Cribs (as available)	No Charge for Children in Parents' Room
Best Western	(800) 528-1234	nominal fee	usually under 12 yrs.
Budgetel Inn	(800) 428-3438	not available	under 18 yrs.
Days Inn	(800) 325-2525	free	under 2 yrs.
Econ-O-Inn	(800) 641-1000	free	under 13 yrs.
Exel Inn	(800) 356-8013	free to $3	under 12 yrs.
Family Inn	(800) 251-9752	$4–$5	varies
Friendship Inn	(800) 453-4511	free to $4	varies
Holiday Inn	(800) 238-8000	free	under 12 yrs. (sometimes for teens)
Howard Johnson	(800) 654-2000	free	under 18 yrs. (where available)
Hyatt	(800) 228-9000	free	under 18 yrs.
Marriott	(800) 228-9290	free	under 18 yrs.
Penny Pincher Inn	(800) 848-5767	free	under 18 yrs.
Radisson	(800) 228-9822	free	under 18 yrs.
Ramada Inn	(800) 228-2828	free	under 18 yrs.
Red Carpet Inn	(800) 251-1962	$3–$5	varies
Red Roof Inn	(800) 848-7878	free	under 18 yrs.
Rodeway Inn	(800) 228-2000	free	under 17 yrs.
Sheraton	(800) 325-3535	free/or a fee	under 18 yrs.
Super 8 Motel	(800) 843-1991	free to $4	varies
Thrifty Scot Motel	(800) 228-3222	$3	varies
TraveLodge	(800) 255-3050	free	under 17 yrs.

• Consider two rooms, if your budget allows; everyone may sleep better. If you have two adults, book two rooms as singles with a child for each adult. You can save 25 to 40 percent on your room rates this way. Obviously, connecting rooms are best, but if that's not possible, you may want to bring a room intercom. (See page 36.)

- Check into the possibility of a two-room suite (a bedroom and living room with convertible beds in the living room). The cost may be the same as, or even less than, that for two rooms.

- Ask if there is a special rate for adjoining rooms.

- Request the last two rooms in a section. If the children are in the end room, near drink dispensers, laundries, or staircases, you will have less worry about the noise they make.

Beyond Hotels and Motels

You may also wish to investigate the possibilities of villas, town houses, or condominiums that offer comfort, privacy, and kitchen/laundry facilities.

Exchange houses or apartments with a family in another state, across country, or in another country so you'll have a comfortable home away from home.

Exchange-a-Home Information

Vacation Exchange Club
12006 111th Ave., Suite 12
Youngtown, AZ 85363
(602) 972-2186

International Home Ex-
    change
250 Bel Marin Keys
Ignacio, CA 94947
(415) 383-7368

Holiday Exchanges
P.O. Box 5294
Ventura, CA 93003
(805) 642-4879

Home Exchange Interna-
    tional
22458 Ventura Blvd., Suite E
Woodland Hills, CA 91364
(818) 992-8990

World Wide Exchanges
P.O. Box 1563
San Leandro, CA 94577
(415) 521-7890

Or rent another family's home. Travel agents and chambers of commerce or local newspapers' classified ads are good leads. There are also organizations to check with. When writing to the services listed, indicate the number of people in your party, the number of children and their ages, your price range, and any specialized interests you have.

Rent-a-Home Information

At-Home Abroad
405 E. 56th Street, #6H
New York, NY 10022
(212) 421-9165

Travel Resources
P.O. Box 1043
Coconut Grove, FL 33133
(800) 327-5039

Rent Abroad
P.O. Box 5183
Westport, CT 06880
(203) 227-9376

Villa Leisure
P.O. Box 1096
Fairfield, CT 06430
(203) 222-9611

Caribbean Home Rental
P.O. Box 710
Palm Beach, FL 33480
(305) 833-4454

If you are interested in "bed and breakfast" accommodations, let any place you contact know you have a child (or children) with you. Some houses don't accept children for reasons ranging from personal preference to concern over care of antique furnishings.

Arranging for Baby-Sitters

By the time you reach your destination, you and your spouse may be more than ready for a night (or an afternoon) out on the town away from the kids. Some family-oriented hotels, motels, and resorts have off-duty staff members available for sitting, and others provide lists of recommended sitters. You may even be able to get your hotel's cooperation in arranging for a sitter before you arrive. Rates vary according to locale, and you will probably be responsible for providing transportation.

Working parents who must be away for a day or two at a time and who find separation from a child difficult have discovered that occasional traveling with a child provides quality time that's otherwise hard to come by. Daytime sitters can be arranged for ahead of time (the better the hotel, the better your chances will be) so parent and child can have a late-afternoon excursion and dinner together.

Not every place will have or recommend sitters, and well-traveled parents have devised other ways to locate one.

- Look in the Yellow Pages under "Baby-Sitters," "Child Care," or "Sitters" to find a listing of agencies. These sitters are carefully screened; some are insured and bonded. Rates are higher because an agency is involved.

- Call a church or day-care center and ask for suggestions for reliable, qualified sitters.

- Call a high school, hospital nursing school, or business school. Many schools post part-time jobs as a service to their students. Ask for at least one reference, and *check it out.*

- Be open to asking local parents you meet (go out of your way to do so if necessary) for names of reliable sitters in their locale.

- Look for fellow "family travelers" with teenagers. These teens often are happy to earn a little vacation spending money by baby-sitting.

- Consider taking a teenage sitter with you, if your budget allows, to help entertain your child or children and to give the adults a chance to get away occasionally. Many teens are delighted with the idea of a trip. Your main expense for the teen will be for food and lodging. Be sure the sitter knows exactly when he or she will be on duty and when on his or her own.

Since they were born, I've taken my children on various business trips to condition them to travel and the business world. Business associates usually have daycare or sitters to recommend. I'm able to stay out on the road longer, and the children realize trips are normal events that one leaves on and returns from.
Susan DeNuccio, North Oaks, MN

2

Packing

❧

When you travel with children, having the right equipment with you can make the difference between a great trip and a so-so one. The trick is to take just enough to cover your needs, but not so much that you can't carry it conveniently. Some things you can do without, and if you can't fit in something you need (or if you forget it), you can probably buy it at your destination—or better yet, rent it!

Packing for Baby

If you were surprised to find how much equipment your new infant needed at home, you may be surprised again to find how much of it is essential when you travel, even for a weekend. Diapers come to mind first, and obviously disposables are easiest. There's more, though, lots more: all the little clothes, the feeding paraphernalia, the absolutely basic equipment . . . and all those things it would be *nice* to have with you.

Basic Baby Baggage

Your baby bag—that ubiquitous carry-all—should have a waterproof lining and a shoulder strap. If you choose a good one and pack it right, it will serve for everything from short trips to extended vacation travel. Some baby bags come with a side that extends and can be used as a changing pad.

If fashion isn't important to you, a backpack makes a very practical baby bag.

Minimum Carry-all Inventory

- Disposable diapers (one to four).
- Disposable wipes or tissues (or dampened paper towel/washcloth kept in a resealable plastic bag).
- Sample-size containers of powder, cream, lotion, and other necessities.
- Extra pacifier (if child is addicted).
- Food, formula, water, and/or juice (with appropriate extra bottles and nipples).
- Change of clothes (one to three).
- Bib or cloth diaper for cover-up.
- "The Versatile, All-Purpose Baby Blanket."
- Plastic bags for disposables or laundry.

To prevent leaks, pack medicines, toiletries, and liquid vitamins in resealable plastic bags before putting them in your baby bag.

You may also want to keep a two-foot square of plastic or vinyl (or even a square of washable wallpaper) in your bag to place under your baby for diaper changes. You can buy commercial changing pads for this purpose, too.

Always keep your baby bag stocked and ready to go. Don't wait until you need it. This way you'll always be ready to take off—a very free feeling.

A roll of plastic sandwich bags in the diaper bag comes in handy for everything from a wet diaper to a sandwich. I always forget to replace a bread bag or other single plastic bag, but the roll is always there— a real lifesaver!

Susan Miller, Wyoming, MI

Warm and Cozy

- Take stretch suits that cover a baby from neck to toe. They're compact, they rinse out easily, and they afford protection from sun and insects.

- Use blanket sleepers for nighttime and forget about blankets.

Luggage Logic

For longer trips, you'll need more than a baby bag, of course. Don't just toss things into suitcases and duffel bags. *Where* you pack things can be almost as important as *what* you pack. If something isn't available when you need it, it's almost as bad as not having it at all. A snack in the cooler at the bottom of your car trunk does no one any good if you are on an interstate highway and can't stop.

- Remove disposable diapers from boxes and stash them in the corners of suitcases or tote bags if you are trying to cut down on luggage.

- Plan on taking not less than three complete outfits, even if you're traveling light: one to wear, one in the laundry, one in reserve.

- Put your baby's clothes on top of yours if you are sharing a suitcase. They'll be easier to reach.

- Pack all the baby clothes in one suitcase. Keep outfits— T-shirt, pants, shirt, and socks—together to save time when you need a change of clothes. If you're *really* organized, you could pack each outfit in its own plastic bag.

- Line your suitcase with plastic garbage bags, which will keep your clothes free from outside moisture and provide you with bags that will come in handy for everything from packing laundry to lining bed mattresses. (**Warning:** Never let children play with plastic bags. They can be dangerous and cause suffocation.)

The Versatile, All-Purpose Baby Blanket

Use it:
- As a changing pad.
- To cover a spot for napping.
- As a "lovey."
- For a nursing cover-up.
- As the right size coverlet for a crib away from home.
- Folded, for a baby's head rest.
- To pad a car seat or infant seat.
- As a good "floor area" for baby play.

Basic Baby Equipment for Travel

A car seat that can double as an infant seat (*never* the reverse!). See page 80 for information on car seats acceptable for airplane travel.

A soft front- or back-carrier or a hip-sling. Look for a style that fits your taste, budget, and life-style. They are wonderful for traveling with infants and can be used at home in a variety of situations.

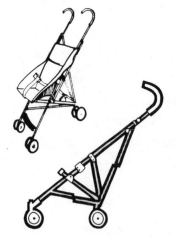

A collapsible stroller. The umbrella style probably is the lightest and can be used by a baby not yet able to sit up. Many new ones have optional features (such as a windguard) that may be of interest to you.

A hard-frame backpack carrier. Suitable only for babies about 6 months and older, because good back and neck control are required. They can be used somewhat earlier if you pad and support the baby with blankets or towels. Some have "loading" frames that allow them to be used (with caution) as feeding chairs or stand-up sleepers.

Using Your Backpack to Best Advantage

- "Practice" with your backpack before you go on any extended trip so both you and your baby find your comfort and endurance level. Comfort level for baby and adult should be at least up to an hour or it's not worth taking. Also make sure your baby can be comfortable when he or she falls asleep in the backpack.

- Wrap pipe insulation around the frame of a backpack to make it more comfortable to wear.

- If your pack doesn't have a special compartment, you can still stash spare disposable diapers under baby's bottom.

- Carry a small mirror in your pocket, to use as a "rearview mirror" to check on your baby.

- Think of investing in a specially made snowsuit that has legs but a blanket-type top instead of sleeves. They work well in backpacks in cold weather. Inquire about the Baby Bag® from Good Gear for Little People, Washington, ME 04574, (207) 845-2211, or the Down Baby Bag from The Company Store, 1205 South 7th St., La Crosse, WI 54601, (800) 356-9367.

Wonderful Optional Equipment

What you take, beyond the bare necessities, will depend on how you travel (obviously a car will allow you to tote more than a plane will), how old your child is, and how willing you and your spouse are to carry extra paraphernalia. Many parents say that less is better, despite the fact that there is comfort in being well equipped. Some items to consider:

- Straw basket baby bed or portable carrying bed
- Portable, collapsible crib
- Portable hanging high chair (see page 50 for information)
- Walker that can double as a high chair
- Baby swing that takes up little room when collapsed
- Jolly Jumper, to hang from a doorway or a tree
- Baby-food grinder (many consider this item mandatory)
- Thermos (wide-mouth is most useful)
- Room intercom

If you are going by car, pack the night before!

Packing for Your Toddler

Double everything you need for an infant and you'll be approaching the minimum of your toddler's needs. These sometimes restive travelers get wetter and dirtier than babies, so they need more clothes. They get hungrier, so they need frequent snacks and meals. And they need the distractions that toys, books, and games offer. If you've passed the early stages of potty training, you may need fewer diapers, but you'll probably have some alternate gear to tote.

Additional Take-along Items

- Clip clothespins for attaching clothes to hangers or to drip-dry clothes overnight.
- Mild soap and baby shampoo. (In a pinch, you can use the shampoo for hand laundry.)
- A flashlight and/or matches and candles.
- A night light to make getting up in the night easier and so your child can see where he or she is during the night.
- An extension cord—locations of hotel outlets are notoriously inconvenient.
- An electric fry pan or hot pot for quick meals in your room.
- A can opener, a paring knife, and a bottle opener (or just a Swiss Army knife).
- A small sewing kit and scissors.
- A roll of masking tape to repair disposable diapers (also a good lint remover).

And don't forget your camera!

- Keep nonperishable finger foods on hand for hunger, teething relief, or distraction. (See page 44 for ideas.)

- Take childproofing equipment such as electrical-outlet covers if you'll be staying at a hotel or in the home of someone who might not have them.

- Pack a few familiar items from home to help ease the "travel trauma" experienced by some youngsters. The regular nighttime security blanket, bedtime doll, or stuffed animal is *essential*.

- Take a *new* toy, however small.

- Make easy washability the main consideration when choosing clothes, and choose clothes that don't show dirt.

- Consider packing extra shoelaces for your child's shoes.

- Bring a high-chair strap (or carry an elastic belt to use as one) to keep a "climber" in place when eating out.

- Select travel clothing with an eye to layering so you'll be prepared for sudden changes in the weather. Sweaters can be an important item.

Specials for the Newly Potty-Trained

Some children are entranced with the idea of using unfamiliar toilet facilities; others find them scary. If you know you'll be traveling, it's a good idea to encourage use of unfamiliar facilities whenever you are out and about.

- Take a potty seat or a toilet-seat adapter along. (A plastic adapter that folds down to a five-inch-square purse size is available from Practical Parenting, Deephaven, MN 55391 for $5.50 postpaid.)

- Consider keeping your potty chair in the car, or take a camping portable potty to eliminate the need to find a rest room—when you've just passed a rest stop and there won't be another for fifteen miles.

- Let little boys use a jar or can for urinating in the car, but not while the car is moving. A plastic ice-cream bucket can work for little girls if you ensure a good "fit." Always pull over for potty stops.

- Pack a waterproof sheet, small plastic tablecloth, or heavy plastic bag to cover mattresses. Hotel staff will be just as appreciative as relatives and friends. Remember, diapers

have been known to leak (and so have toilet-trained toddlers!).

• Don't hesitate to go back to diapers for nighttime or even
daytime use if your child regresses. Worry about training
or retraining when you get back home rather than making
your trip a battleground.

Traveling Toys

Infants don't need the distractions of toys, but infancy passes,
and soon you will find yourself taking toys as well as tots.
Older toddlers will want to pick their own favorites to travel
with. Within reason, this is a good idea, but don't rely on a
child to pick the most appropriate toys. Let him or her select
some favorites, and choose the rest yourself. Don't let your
toddler persuade you to take along a talking or musical toy.
Any repetitive sound in close quarters will quickly drive all
within earshot up the wall.

The smaller the toys, the more variety you'll have room for.
Yet, "small" can be a choking hazard for your child. Also,
small toys are more easily lost, dropped, and caught in tight
places.

And remember that many cities now have toy libraries. You
can call your local library branch for such information if it is
not found easily in your phone book.

• Include soft toys to hug, cuddle, and sleep with.

• Stash crayons, coloring books, and other nonmessy art
supplies in a cake pan with a lid. The closed pan can serve
as a work surface. A cookie sheet works well, too, and
magnetized toys or puzzles can be used on both.

• Bring along Bristle Blocks® or other large-size, snap-
together plastic construction toys. If you lose one or two,
it won't be a big loss.

- Make a surprise package by wrapping several toys and books with lots of string and tape. Let the child select one when things get tense.

- Pack a special bag for each child and fill it with surprises and special favorites. An old attaché case makes a good carrying case.

- Bring hand puppets to entertain a child when restlessness sets in. A puppet "eating" a small, deflated balloon looks as if it is blowing bubbles.

- Blowing up balloons can provide good entertainment if there's an extra adult in the car. Keep them small, or let the air whistle out, draw faces on the balloons, or tie one to a car seat. (Never let a child chew on broken pieces of balloons because there are chemicals on the inside of the pieces, and the pieces can cause choking.)

About two weeks before a trip I hide some favorite toys and even buy a few new ones. When boredom sets in, I give my son a "surprise" to open.
Wendy Lazear, Deephaven, MN

- Don't forget the Magic Slate®! It can provide hours of fun with no mess and eliminates the need for excess paper. It probably will get ripped along the way, but then it will be one less thing to carry home.

- Consider swapping some old toys with a friend or neighbor or borrowing some, so you'll have a few that are really new to your children.

- Bring along a list of (and maybe the words to) some favorite songs: "If You're Happy and You Know It," "This Old

Man," "Three Blind Mice," "It Ain't Gonna Rain," or "Do Your Ears Hang Low?," for example. Or pick up one of the *Wee Sing* song books (Los Angeles: Price/Stern/Sloan) with or without the accompanying tape cassettes.

- Above all, carry *books, books,* and *more books* to read to your child while you're traveling, while you're waiting in restaurants, before bedtime.

- Remember that *you* will always be your child's favorite toy.

Bubbles! At any age kids like them. They're so small and transparent they don't block the driver's view. They're inexpensive, and if they spill, the worst that happens is you have one clean spot on the seat or the floor.

Sandi Mink, Detroit, MI

The Modern Technology of Tapes

- Take children's tapes to play in a car's tape deck or a child's cassette player. Or a small portable cassette player with headphones for the child old enough to use them.

- Buy picture books accompanied by tapes.

- Tape stories and songs yourself before you leave, and check out others from the library.

- You can record a story as you read it in the car and your child can play it back and read along with the book.

- Include a few blank tapes to record some of your travel experiences, or songs or stories.

- Bring along extra batteries for portable tape cassettes.

Cassette Catalogues
to Send For

In addition to tapes and book-tape sets you can find in stores or libraries, the following companies sell a variety of excellent cassettes by mail.

Children's Recordings
P.O. Box 11032
Eugene, OR 97440
(503) 485-1634

Linden International
365 1st St.
Los Altos, CA 94022
(415) 949-3390

Educational Record Center
472 East Paces Ferry Rd.
Atlanta, GA 30305
(404) 233-5935

Children's Book and Music
   Center
2500 Santa Monica Blvd.
Santa Monica, CA 90404
(213) 829-0215

Educational Activities
P.O. Box 392
Freeport, NY 11520
(516) 223-4666

Metacom Free Catalogue
1401B W. River Rd.
Minneapolis, MN 55411
(612) 588-2781

Especially for Car Travel

- Tie small toys (preferably soft ones) to your child's car restraint so they won't get lost in the car and you won't have to hunt for them constantly.

- Stretch an elastic cord (with hooks on each end) between the clothes hooks on each side of the back seat and tie soft toys within reach of the child's car seat.

- Keep some of the toys in the trunk, and stop occasionally to trade an old toy for an unfamiliar one.

- Pack a few toys in a small box that will fit between two children's car restraints in the back seat so both can reach them.

- Include a toy telephone. They're wonderful for holding pretend conversations between cars.

- For rest stops, remember toys such as inflatable beach balls, balloons, and, for older children, jump ropes.

> Books, Lego®, Etch-a-Sketch®, and Colorform®-type stickers for the car windows help keep my children occupied. Songs and frequent stops are important.
> *Becky Gammons, Beaverton, OR*

- Make a lap tray for a child in a car seat. A folding bed tray probably won't fit, but you can make one from a sturdy box. If you're handy, make a wooden one with hinges for folding sides. Be sure to have a raised edge at the front to keep toys from rolling off.

- Bring an empty scrapbook for your toddler to fill with postcards, brochures, and other mementos of the trip. Keep your eye out for things to put in this memory book.

3

Sleeping Away from Home

🌷

Sleeping away from home is easiest with a new baby, though we most often hesitate to travel with an infant because of the newness of the situation and all the upheaval already caused by the baby. But babies can and do sleep anywhere.

After your baby is 6 months old, it will be harder to sleep "just anywhere" due to his or her growing mobility and the fact that travel now will probably begin to affect sleep patterns. After 1 year of age, your child will be familiar enough with his or her own bedroom to be aware of and stimulated by different surroundings. If you've sheltered your child from changes in environment and schedules, travel may be more disruptive.

It's a good idea to get your baby used to sleeping and eating in different places as early as possible, so all the adjusting won't have to be done during the trip. Before you leave, have your child try sleeping in different rooms in the house or apartment. Make a game of it for a toddler.

Mentally program yourself to accept a child who won't take a nap or go to bed at the usual time. Understand that your child will sleep when tired, and try to forget your usual schedule. Accept whatever comes as your new routine and you will be much more at ease. When you get home, you can get your child back to a more predictable sleeping schedule once again.

Settling In

What, for you, is a routine trip may be, for your child, an exciting adventure that *can't* be missed, even for sleep. Since a good night's sleep can help ensure the success of the following day, do everything you can to make your child feel comfortable and secure at night.

Unfortunately, an overtired child does not necessarily go to sleep faster or stay asleep or sleep longer despite the logic of the situation.

What Is a Bed?

If you haven't brought your own portable crib or small playpen along, you can arrange for a crib to be set up in a hotel/motel room before you arrive so a sleeping baby can be put right to bed. If the baby is awake, the crib provides a place to put him or her safely while you unload and unpack. If the place at which you'll be staying doesn't supply a crib and you'll be there for any length of time, arrange to rent a crib from a rental agency. There are a variety of small, collapsible beds (and even some inflatable ones) in stores or listed in mail-order catalogues.

But a bed (defined only as where your baby will sleep) can be improvised easily and eliminates the need for extra items to carry.

- Make a bed for an infant in a padded drawer or laundry basket placed on the floor. A pillow with a towel wrapped securely around it makes a good pad.

- Make a "nest" for an infant (but only one who can't turn over yet) on an unused big bed by surrounding the infant with pillows and extra blankets rolled up (and, of course, with a waterproof pad underneath).

- Or place a small inflatable wading pool on top of a bed. Line it with a soft towel or blanket.

- Make a low hammock for a baby by tucking the ends of a sheet between the mattresses of two beds spaced about three feet apart. Place a pillow or cushion on the floor under the sheet to make it more comfortable. Baby rests on the cushioned floor, and the hammock sides keep away drafts.

Other Improvisations

- Let your child sleep with you in your bed if you are used to the family bed system. Or let your child fall asleep in the family bed, then move the child to his or her own bed once asleep.

- If you have more than one child, position them sideways on a double bed. That will increase their "sprawl" expanse.

- Push against a wall the bed your child will use, and place chairs against the remaining sides to prevent roll-offs.

- Bring along a bedrail that secures between the mattress and the box spring, to provide extra security for a toddler unaccustomed to sleeping in a strange bed. Some vacation spots have bedrails.

Getting Children to Sleep in Hotels/Motels

Whatever your sleeping arrangements, be prepared to take extra time to get your child to sleep. Sometimes it's necessary to turn off the light and wait outside in the hall until a child settles down. Once your child is asleep, you and your spouse can take turns going for a swim, a cup of coffee, or a stroll. Or make your own private time in the room together by watching TV softly or playing an adult game brought along for just these moments.

- Help a baby fall asleep by putting the crib against the window and closing the drapes around the outside of the crib. When you go to bed, put the drapes back against the window so the morning light doesn't wake the baby.

- Camp out in the bathroom after your child is in bed. Use the bathroom time for personal grooming.

- Let a TV or radio help lull a child to sleep.

Making Your Room Comfortable and Safe

- Consider bringing along your own crib bedding. Most places provide too-large linens that don't "stay put." Your own baby blanket will also be especially useful here.

- Use a spread or an extra blanket from a bed to improvise a bumper pad for a crib if one is not supplied.

- Check the safety features in your room if you have a busy toddler: electrical outlets, loose or dangling cords, windows (if there are no screens, keep them locked), lamps that can be pulled over—everything you've already checked and corrected at home.

- Remember that you *can* move and rearrange furniture to suit *your* needs. Just return it to its original position before you check out.

- Keep your room as tidy as you can for both comfort and efficiency in getting up and on your way to a day's travel or fun. If you'll be in the hotel for more than a couple of nights, unpack clothing and store suitcases in the closet.

- Use a clean wastebasket for a toy chest if clothing takes up all the drawer space.

Listening In

Room intercoms are wonderful items for parents who travel. They are good for:

- Visiting at a relative's house when the baby is sleeping in a distant room.
- Keeping tabs on older children if you can't get adjoining rooms in a hotel/motel.
- Allowing you to be outside while your baby is sleeping inside without the constant need to run in and check.
- Knowing if another child is "checking" on your baby, which might be inappropriate or even unsafe.
- Having at home to check on your sleeping baby.

Intercoms come in two parts. The transmitter is placed near the sleeping baby, and the receiver is placed wherever it's convenient for you. Each part must be plugged into an electrical outlet. Some intercoms have a receiver that also works on batteries, so you can carry it with you. Another type uses your own radio as the receiver.

Receiving-only intercoms cost from $25 to $35. Intercoms that allow you to talk and receive cost between $40 and $60. Check with a local retail electronics store.

Visiting Friends and Relatives

Staying with people you know can be the greatest and simplest vacation or visit, or the most difficult and trickiest; depending upon how adaptable both families are and, probably, on your host family's experience with children.

Remember that if there isn't an infant or toddler in the house, you'll be responsible for whatever childproofing measures are necessary for your own children's safety. Some grandparents will be comfortable childproofing their homes. Others don't feel it fits for them. Don't take lack of interest in childproofing as an insult. You too may feel differently about infants in your home twenty years from now.

> Each gift-giving holiday we give Grandma and Grandpa a toy of the kids' choice for them to keep at their house, thus building an entertainment supply for visits. Grandpa was especially pleased last Christmas when he received a Cookie Monster target game with Velcro balls!
>
> *Vickie Ploucher, Kalamazoo, MI*

Making Yourselves Welcome

- Take a baby blanket to make a spot for play or napping.

- Ask for an old, large bath towel or a sheet of plastic or newspaper to put under a high chair—especially if you are eating in a carpeted room.

- Bring along a waterproof sheet (or flannel-backed pad or tablecloth) to protect surfaces when changing your baby, and also to protect mattresses.

- Protect a tablecloth by putting a plastic place mat under your child's setting.

- Plan some family time together *away* from your hosts to give them a break and some privacy.

- Clean up your own messes.

For a Place You Visit Regularly or for an Extended Period

- Leave an extra bottle, nipple, pacifier, or any other items that are inexpensive enough to duplicate and don't take up a lot of room.

- Buy a used portable crib or a gently used crib, possibly from a store that specializes in children's used furniture. Repaint it (with unleaded, nontoxic paint) for a new look.

- Rent a portable crib in advance from a rental company at your destination. Rental companies often are near airports. Or ask your hosts to arrange this, and reimburse them when you arrive.

- Arrange in advance for a weekly diaper service.

- Arrange to borrow or rent a car restraint if you'll be arriving by plane and you don't want to carry your own. Be sure that it is at the airport when you're being picked up. Or rent a car from a major company, as they often can reserve car seat restraints in advance.

4

Eating Out and En Route

It's important to be flexible about *when* you eat. Missed meals can be compensated for by several healthy snacks, even if this doesn't fit your notion of what a meal should be. As reassuring as schedules are, sometimes they need to be disregarded. Close attention to your child's signals of hunger and boredom is the key to keeping your mobile family comfortable.

If it's at all possible, take a bottle, snack, or mini-meal with you wherever you go. That way you can offer the favored and familiar—important to a good trip for a baby or toddler. Even if your toddler eats table foods, it's wise to have a jar or two of his or her favorite prepared baby food at the bottom of your bag. These don't have to be refrigerated, and they are good insurance.

> **Children behave best when their stomachs
> are full and their bladders are empty.**

Feeding the Baby

Since formula or breast milk is all your infant needs for the first four to six months, your limited menu selection simplifies travel needs.

If you are thinking about weaning your baby from the breast or the bottle in preparation for the trip, think again. Nursing or bottle feeding will provide continuity for your child, and a major change such as weaning during your trip could have the reverse effect from what you had wished.

Nursing Etiquette

Fortunately today it is no longer necessary to banish yourself to a hidden corner if you're nursing.

- Learn how to nurse your baby in your front-pack carrier. Practice at home.

- Drape a light blanket or cloth diaper over your shoulder and over the baby's head while nursing. An attractive shawl or poncho also works well.

- Cover yourself with a large towel or terry robe when at the beach.

- Look in maternity stores for special tops with concealed openings for nursing mothers.

- Or wear blouses, sweaters, or T-shirts that can be lifted at the waist; they're more discreet than tops that button down the center. If you wear a button-down top, unbutton from the bottom for the same effect.

- Try wearing a normal stretch bra for nursing. It's easier to lift one than to unhook a nursing bra.

- Remember that patterned tops hide leaks better than solids do.

- Don't nurse your baby while the car is moving unless you absolutely *must,* and if you must, it's safer in the back seat. It is possible to nurse while both mother and baby are restrained. With your baby in a rear-facing car restraint, you can lean forward toward your baby while still using your own shoulder harness.

- Be sensitive to the fact that there will be people who will be uncomfortable if you nurse in a public place.

- Don't feel you must nurse in public if you are uncomfortable doing it there.

Bottles and Solids

- Treat yourself to some bottled, ready-to serve formula that doesn't need refrigeration. It's more expensive but very convenient. Take sterilized water in the same size bottles for a thirsty (not hungry) baby.

- Carry plastic (not glass) baby bottles to avoid the mess and danger of a broken bottle.

- Put liquid or powdered formula into your bottles or disposable plastic bags in advance and close securely until needed. (Use four scoops of powdered formula to eight ounces of water, or follow instructions on the container.)

- Carry dry milk for a bottle-fed toddler no longer on formula. Put ⅓ cup or 2⅔ ounces in a bottle and add water to make 8 ounces when you're ready to feed the baby.

- Consider buying bottle "straws" that fit into bottle nipples even before your baby can sit upright alone or hold his or her own bottle. These "straws" allow a baby to hold a bottle without tilting the head back and gulping in troublesome air bubbles.

- Bring along a wide-mouth thermos filled with hot water—great for warming up a bottle and helpful for cleanups.

- Pack instant baby cereal, premixed with powdered formula or dry milk, in separate, reclosable plastic bags. When you stop to eat, just pull out one of the packets. Add warm water and serve.

- Keep the baby's food at just the right temperature on a short trip by storing the food in an insulated six-pack bag. Or heat small (4-ounce) unopened jars of baby food and place them inside a 10-ounce wide-mouth thermos.

- Pack the baby's long-handled feeding spoon in a plastic toothbrush case and keep it handy in your purse or diaper bag. Bring an extra spoon in case you lose one. Or just tape a small baby spoon to a jar of baby food.

- Consider mixing some puréed foods or baby cereal with your bottle of formula or milk to make an easy-to-serve meal.

- Bring along your baby-food grinder so your baby can share appropriate food from your plate at a restaurant or at someone else's house.

My daughter has been boating and fishing with us since she was 3 weeks old. I take only necessities and improvise with what is available—a can of Similac can warm in the sun, and so can jars of food. She loves it!

Ann Kooperman, Turnersville, NJ

Eating on the Go

Bringing food from home—and restocking along the way, if your trip is long—are terrific solutions to the problem of eating on the go.

You save money and you can have more control over the family's diet by bringing along a well-stocked cooler. Commercial freezer packs are a good dripless investment, or pack ice cubes in heavy-duty freezer bags to keep melting water from leaking. A good insulated food carrier small enough to fit beneath feet will be helpful.

Many gas stations or convenience stores have ice cubes when you need them.

Traveling and snacking go hand in hand, so don't be *too* concerned about diet.

> **Unfortunately, the things that make them the happiest are gum and food—the messier, the better. By the end of the week, the back seat and floor of the car could easily feed a family of five. If no one's screaming or fighting, who cares?**
> *Cynthia Carlton, Los Angeles, CA*

Food, Food!

- Tie a bagel to the car seat with a string for a toddler. It's better than an all-day sucker.

- Keep crackers and cookies fresh by putting them in a covered plastic container.

- Bring along a can of "squirt" cheese to serve on crackers.

- Serve a container of yogurt with a straw inserted through the top lid for a spillproof snack or meal.

- Use an old shoe box lined with aluminum foil as a plate for a meal-in-a-box.

- Beware of foods that might cause a child to choke or gag. Having an adult sit in the back seat with a child who is eating is a good safety precaution.

- Cut down on potty stops by avoiding salty foods that make youngsters drink more.

- Pack disposable items such as paper plates, cups, forks, spoons, and wipes. Remember—the trick to easy traveling is to cut down on your cleanup time.

- Eat lunches and snacks at rest stops when you can, so everyone can get out of the car and get some fresh air and exercise.

- Pack snacks individually in resealable small plastic bags to make handing out food faster and easier.

Safe Toddler Snacks

- cheese slices or chunks; string cheese
- bananas
- seedless grapes (cut in half for babies under 1 year)
- other fruit (cut up)
- crackers
- bagels or frozen bagel sticks
- pretzels (preferably unsalted)
- dry cereal
- small cut-up sandwiches

Remember that ice cubes and small, hard foods should be avoided for small children. Choking can be impossible to deal with while the car is in motion.

Satisfying Thirst

- To cut down on pit stops, take water rather than other more "interesting" drinks. Kids probably will drink water only when they're really thirsty, rather than just because they like the taste.

- Make an X-shaped slit in a baby bottle nipple. When your toddler gets thirsty, invert the nipple inside the bottle and put a straw through the slit to make a spillproof (well, almost) container.

- Try boxed drinks with straws for toddlers—they love them. Although they're not entirely spillproof, they are usually neat, and they're disposable.

WARNING
Watch a child using a straw in a car.
The straw could cause injury in case of
a quick stop.

- Take collapsible drinking cups to use in the car and at drinking fountains that small children can't reach.

- Or try the small, narrow Tupperware® cups that have re-sealable nonspill covers and also fit a small child's hand.

- Look for the children's thermos bottles with special spouts for a straw.

- Fill a plastic jug half or three-quarters full with water. Freeze it. When you're ready to go, fill the jug to the top with tap water. The water will remain cold, and as the ice melts you will have additional cold water to drink. The jug can also double as an ice pack for your cooler.

- Never bring a drink that will stain if you spill it. *You* will and *it* will!

45

The greatest snacks we have carried are oranges. I carry a paring knife and a small paper bag for easy peeling and disposal of trash. The oranges satisfy both hunger and thirst, and the citrus helps combat car sickness.

Mrs. Donald Thompson, Louisa, KY

We hang our two children's Yogi Bear canteens from the garment hooks on each side of the back seat, filled with each one's favorite drink. When it's gone, they get no more, so they learn to sip.

Mrs. J. Putnam, Claremont, NH

I put a drink in one of those empty plastic lemon/lime dispensers so my daughter can just squeeze it in her mouth and replace the cap when she's finished. No spills—no mess! And she loves it.

B. Lipman, S. Windham, ME

Dealing with Drips and Spills

- Use absorbent cloth diapers for mopping up spills. Or keep a damp sponge in a plastic bag.

- Keep an extra change of clothes handy for accidents.

- Cover the back seat of a car under your child with a beach towel to catch crumbs. Or put a piece of heavy plastic under the baby's car seat. You can also protect your car upholstery by investing in a heavy-duty rubber "Seat Saver" that fits under all children's car restraints. (For stores that sell the "Seat Saver," write Prince Lionheart, 2301 Cape Cod Way, Santa Ana, CA 92703.)

- Cut slits in the middle of some small paper plates. When it's time for treats such as Popsicles or ice-cream bars, insert the sticks into the slits and let the plate catch the drips (well, at least some of them).

- Bring bibs for feeding your baby on the go. A small terry-cloth towel, secured with diaper pins, works well. Bibs of soft, thin sponge can be rinsed and reused, and they also make good wipes for hands and faces. Bibs can limit dirty laundry caused by constant drool.

Disposable Plastic Bibs

Disposable plastic bibs are good traveling aids. Look for them in the baby section of your local drugstore or discount store. Or order them by mail from:

BIB-AWAY Corp.
P.O. Box 22802
Beachwood, OH 44122

Send $3.49 plus $.75 postage for fifty bibs.

Eating in Restaurants

Finding good places to eat with little ones can be difficult in a strange town. If you know someone who's been where you're going, ask for recommendations. Hotel and motel personnel often are good sources of information, too. Ethnic and family-style restaurants usually are good choices. If you're trying to save money, make breakfast the biggest meal of the day—it's almost always less expensive than lunch or dinner.

Fast-food places may offer outdoor playgrounds and picnic tables, if not the best in well-rounded nutritional selections (which you can supplement, anyway). In addition to their convenience, they usually can be counted on to have clean and fairly spacious rest rooms. Consider choosing a drive-in restaurant if you are traveling with a very fussy baby, or at least pick a noisy restaurant, where you won't be that noticeable!

You can ask any restaurant to fill your thermos with boiling water so that you can mix cereal, soup, or just heat up formula along the way or for breakfast the next day. Many will also restock your water jug with ice cubes.

You can also feed your baby first and then take your satisfied child with you while you enjoy your meal out. Save good adult restaurants for times when you can leave the children with a sitter.

It's wise to call ahead and make dinner reservations if you can and to check on the availability of high chairs, booster seats, and children's menus. Try to keep your meal schedule as close as possible to the one you follow at home, but eat early, rather than late, both to avoid the crowds and to keep the children happy and satisfied.

You might want to dress your children in their pajamas at your dinner stop when you're traveling by car. This allows you to have them ready for bed when you arrive so they can be tucked in with minimum fuss.

The Young and the Restless

- Be sensitive and flexible about suitable placement of an infant seat. It will take up a lot of room on a restaurant table and can be in the way on the floor. A booth can be a good choice as a place for eating with a child in an infant seat. The seat can fit on the table or the seat.

- Eat out late if you have a baby who can sleep through the activity. Let the baby sleep in a carrier or on a pile of coats on the floor beneath the table.

- Let a baby play with an ice cube on the high-chair tray. It's good fun until it melts. *Don't* give your baby a metal spoon or fork to bang on a metal tray. It does nothing for other diners' digestion (or their eardrums)!

- Wait for the food to arrive before putting a baby in a high chair, but don't let a walking child circulate. It's dangerous, and it's annoying to other diners.

- Let your toddler sit in a seat facing a window. Cars and people will provide distraction. If you can't get a window seat, at least sit by a wall, to be out of the way.

- Keep a booster seat in your car for use in an unaccommodating restaurant. You can make a homemade seat from old catalogues wrapped in contact paper. Or your car restraint can act as a booster seat in a booth.

Portable Hanging High Chairs

These high chairs, which attach to most tables, can be wonderful for travelers with small children, and many parents even opt to use these at home to save space. They are compact and can usually accommodate children up to forty pounds. Leverage makes these chairs work, and they are safe if the table is stable.

Some of these models now come with table trays, removable fabric seat covers, and safety straps. Some fold up, others do not. Most cost about $20 to $25.

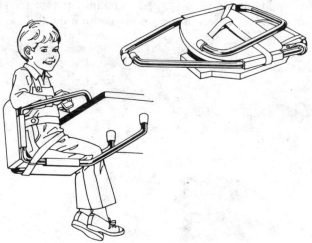

Check for stability before attaching the chair; round pedestal tables tend to tip over easily. In addition, check to see that your child's feet cannot reach anything nearby, so he or she can't "push off," especially possible with a picnic table over a bench or a booth table in a restaurant.

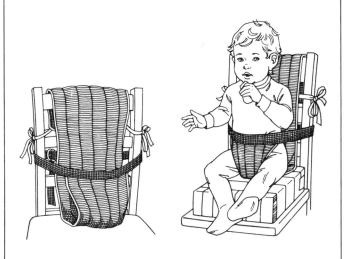

Or you may prefer, for traveling (or even for home use), a fabric high chair that slips over the back of a chair, although it can be used only on certain types of chairs. The fabric ties around the baby's bottom like a sling and ties around the back of a chair. It is also useful for shopping carts, strollers, and regular high chairs. (Check for availability by writing to: Comfi Baby Products, 5754 Fairlawn Shores, Prior Lake, MN 55372, for The Tie Chair; and Good Gear for Little People, Washington, ME 04574 for The Kiddie Caddie.) If you sew, look for a pattern in a fabric store.

- Avoid booth seats with an unrestrained toddler. (If you don't understand the wisdom of this tip, you will after you sit in a booth with a toddler.)

- Clear the table of condiments, candles, and other attractive nuisances within the reach of a bored child.

- Carry your own "restaurant kit," which might include children's utensils, towelettes, a high-chair strap or belt, large bibs, a few small toys, crayons for drawing on paper place mats or napkins, and even a few crackers. (Ask for a pot of warm water and an extra napkin to clean the table or high-chair tray, if necessary. Or use a moist towelette.)

- Flip a coin to determine which adult will order the meal while the other takes an impatient toddler for a walk until the food arrives.

- If a tantrum occurs and can't be contained, have one adult take the child out while the other waits for the food to be put in doggie bags or other containers. Enjoy a picnic in the hotel room.

Staving Off Hunger

- Let it be known that the children's meals can—and should—be brought first.

- Carry a seven-compartment pillbox (available at drugstores) filled with cereal, raisins, or other small treats. Opening and closing the "doors" will keep your toddler happy for quite a while.

- Ask for crackers or bread to be brought to your table before the main part of the meal, to keep a hungry child quiet.

- Order an appetizer your child can share with you. A chef's salad or fruit platter can be shared, too.

- Bring most or parts of your child's meal with you into the restaurant. Wrap items separately (in aluminum foil, for instance) and let your child open the "presents."

- Ask the restaurant to split an order in the kitchen for a child who is not receptive to eating from the extra plate brought for meal sharing.

- Order a meal with doggie bag potential for a child who is suddenly no longer hungry but will be once you've left the restaurant.

Keeping Cleanup Under Control

- Spread a piece of newspaper or plastic under the high chair of a child you *know* will drop and spill food.

- Bring your child's own training cup to avoid spills.

- Dispose of any opened jars of leftover baby food if you don't have access to a refrigerator or cooler.

- Clean up table messes the children make, and point out any floor spills to a restaurant employee so they can be mopped up promptly.

- Tip helpful restaurant personnel generously!

Eating Where You Stay

Families traveling today make things easier for themselves by packing food to carry from home, buying it where they stay, or bringing in fast-food or other already prepared meals to their rooms. Everybody enjoys the adventure of it all, and the savings in money can be considerable. Having food on hand can be particularly crucial when your toddler wakes up at 6:00 A.M. hungry.

- Have breakfast in your room. You can prepare a hot meal by mixing instant baby cereal with the hottest water from the tap. Provide individual boxes of cold cereal for older tots. The boxes are made to be used as bowls, but put back-up paper plates under them just in case.

- Keep small cans or boxes of juice, crackers, bread, peanut butter, and fresh fruit in your room for quick snacks. Chill juice containers in the ice bucket provided, or bring your own small cooler. Or fill a sink with ice and cover it with towels. Even milk will stay fresh if you keep the ice supply constant.

- Visit a local market or roadside stand and buy fruits or vegetables that can be washed or peeled in your room to supplement meals you bring in.

- Consider using room service for breakfast or dinner. It may not be as expensive as you think, since you can order what you want, and the kids can share single meals. And the mobility it allows the children doesn't have a price tag.

- Let the children "picnic" in the bathtub as an adventure for them and an easy cleanup for you.

5

Going by Car

The family automobile, whether it's a compact car or a full-size van, offers the most privacy and freedom for travel. It also has the advantage of being familiar territory for infants and toddlers who are used to being strapped snugly into a car seat and going places with Mom and Dad. Just be sure to have the car serviced thoroughly before leaving!

If you're a night owl, leave for a long trip about the time your baby usually falls asleep, and drive through the night.

It's often best to travel at night or early in the morning so children can sleep in the car, but don't let them snooze so much that they'll be restless and overly active when you're ready to sleep. Expect to make frequent stops along the way for potty breaks and stretching. In fact, add one-third more to your normal driving time when you're planning your trip.

Plan to end your travel days early. Children find it much easier to go to sleep if they have the opportunity to become familiar with new surroundings. A walk before supper or a dip in the motel pool can set the stage for a calm evening for everyone.

> **We think traveling in a motor home is the only way to go with a 2-year-old. It allows room to move around.**
> *Martha West, Indianola, IA*

Safety Means Car Seats

It is impossible to hold an infant or child safely on your lap in a car. If there is an accident and your child is unrestrained, your arms will offer no protection whatsoever. A car seat is an absolute necessity. The safest position for a car seat is in the middle of the back seat.

You should already have your infant seat by the time you bring your new baby home from the hospital. Improperly restrained babies and children are in jeopardy. Don't use money as an excuse not to have a restraint—the expense is not that great. Isn't your child's life worth the price of two tanks of gasoline or a car radio? Thousands of infants and toddlers are killed or injured each year in car accidents. Sadly, most of these injuries could have been prevented by use of proper seat restraints. If you really can't afford to buy one, take advantage of one of the many rental programs available.

> **Don't use a "car bed"—
> it won't provide adequate protection
> for a baby in an accident.**

Renting a car at your destination? Many major car rental companies now rent children's car seats with their rental cars, depending on the city. Most require a refundable deposit. The seats usually are available only for round-trip rentals. Advance reservations are necessary.

The most important thing to remember is to use an appropriate restraint *every time* your child rides in the car. Make it an unquestionable and inflexible rule. Most states (and several Canadian provinces) now have laws requiring restraints for small children.

Safety Belt Song

(sung to the tune of "Jingle Bells")

Safety Belts, Safety Belts,
Wear them all the way
Every time you're in your car
Any night or day—oh
Safety Belts, Safety Belts,
Put them 'round your lap,
Then before you start to ride,
Everybody—SNAP!

National Safety Council

Baby Comfort and Safety

- A baby *must* ride backward in an infant seat until he or she weighs seventeen to twenty pounds. If you're traveling alone with your baby, connect the infant seat to the car's front safety belt next to you so you can make quick checks on his or her comfort without having to turn your head to the back as you drive.

- Keep a small baby centered in the car seat by tucking small baby blankets or rolled-up diapers between the sides of the seat and the baby's head.

- Make a baby more comfortable by placing a folded blanket under his or her knees so they are slightly bent.

- Have one of two adults ride in the back seat with the baby as an occasional option.

- Adjust harnesses on car restraints as you change the baby's clothing to adjust to weather changes.

Toddler Tactics

- Be sure all fingers are safely out of the way before closing the car doors. Make a game of having all hands reach for the sky, or have your child give himself or herself a hug before you close the door.

- Don't enable a child to play with door locks by putting car seats too close to doors. Hardware and auto stores sell safety locks that fit over standard push-down car door locks.

- Make it a rule that the engine isn't started until everyone is safely restrained. This means adults, too! Use the line "Do you want me to get arrested?"

- The car should come to a complete stop before you unfasten the children's restraints and adults' seat belts.

Common Mistakes Parents Make with Car Restraints for Children

They:

- diligently read everything on childbirth, nutrition, and parenting, yet fail to protect their children by not using the restraints properly every time they are in a car.

- bundle an infant in a blanket, making it impossible to secure the shoulder harness properly. A blanket can be tucked around the baby *after* the belt is buckled.

- forget to secure the seat with the auto lap belt. If the lap belt does not fit around or through the frame, try another position in the car or try another type of seat. Be sure you have followed instructions correctly if you have difficulties.

• neglect to use the shoulder harness, or use it incorrectly. This makes the restraint itself potentially hazardous to a child. Many harnesses are too loose (only two finger widths should fit between the harness and the child's body) or are not threaded through the correct slots in the seat. It's important also to keep the lap portion of the belt low and the crotch snap short to avoid injuries to the child's abdomen.

Bumper stickers from the American Academy of Pediatrics

• neglect to fasten the top anchor strap, when required. Often this is because of uncertainty about how to affix the anchor, or unwillingness to bolt the anchor to the car. The strap must be attached to the rear window ledge, or to the floor of the rear compartment (in a station wagon or hatchback). Toyota was one of the first to equip its entire car line with provisions for easy installation of children's car restraints. Several other manufacturers now offer models with anchor provisions.

59

- let children loose or out of their car restraints when they complain. Children *can* be taught their place in the car.

- don't insist that grandparents, baby-sitters, and other caretakers put children in car seats when they are driving.

- don't wear seat belts themselves. They set a bad example, and risk the possibility of turning their safely-buckled children into orphans.

Safety Also Means . . .

- checking under and behind your car before backing out of your driveway.
- never leaving keys in the ignition while your car is parked.
- feeling the seat and seat-belt buckle on a hot summer day to be sure they will not burn a child's sensitive skin. A towel makes an adequate seat cover on a hot day.
- keeping the dashboard and rear window ledge free of loose objects that could fly off and hit a child if you have to stop suddenly. Even a box of tissues can be a hazard.
- keeping at least one window slightly open to ensure against any danger of carbon monoxide poisoning.
- never leaving a baby or toddler alone in a car.
- confining your pet; a loose dog or cat can be a dangerous distraction.
- locking your car when you get out. Children can climb in, release hand brakes, lock themselves in, and do all kinds of damage.
- locking all doors while traveling.

What to Look for in a Car Restraint

- Make sure it's comfortable. Some seats come with soft new fabric coverings, although they're usually more expensive. You can also purchase a seat cover separately.

- Unpack the restraint in the store to be sure all instructions and parts are included.

- Check to be sure that the restraint is easy to use. It will be fastened and unfastened many times; if it's hard to use, you'll be less likely to use it.

- Check the label to be sure the restraint meets federal requirements. (This means it has flame-retardant padding, childproof buckles, and can withstand 20 mph side and 30 mph front collisions.) All seats produced after January 1981 must meet these standards.

- Make sure the restraint fits your car. Try it in both the front and rear seats. If it doesn't fit, you *can* exchange it! Be sure the restraint doesn't block your rear vision.

- Buy a restraint that doesn't need a tether if you plan to move the restraint between cars.

Keeping Sunlight out of Your Child's Eyes

- Bring a soft toy along that's big enough to shield eyes and can't get lost under the seat.

- Buy a light-filtering sheet of plastic that can be attached to the car windows. It will also prevent the seats from getting hot.

- Use strips of Velcro above a back side window to attach a shade (fabric, blanket) as needed.

Four Kinds of Car Seat Restraints

Infant seats: These are for infants from birth to about 9 months (17 to 20 pounds). They usually recline and are to be used only facing backward.

Convertible infant/toddler seats: These can be positioned backward and tilt backward but can be used turned around and upright when the child gets old enough to fit a toddler car seat. These will cover weight from birth to 40 pounds.

TODDLER POSITION

INFANT POSITION

Toddler seats: These are for children who can sit upright. They are usually appropriate for children 9 months to 4 years old (20 to 40 pounds).

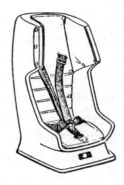

Auto booster seats: These elevate a child who has outgrown the standard seat but still isn't tall enough to see out the window. They work with the shoulder/lap seat belt or with a tether/harness system. Read instructions carefully to see what is required of each model. These seats can double as booster seats in restaurants and elsewhere—but lightweight, inexpensive booster seats should *never* be used as car boosters.

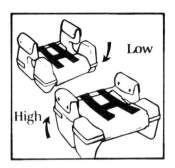

You will probably simply purchase a seat from the choices available in local stores, but if you are interested in a shopping guide to car seat restraints, send a long self-addressed, stamped envelope to: Division of Public Education, American Academy of Pediatrics, P.O. Box 927, Oak Grove, IL 60007, and ask for a copy of "The Family Guide to Infant/Child Automobile Restraints." You may also wish to check the April 1982 issue of *Consumer Reports* or send $2 for the reprint of the article "Child Safety Seats" c/o *Consumer Reports,* P.O. Box 2485, Boulder, CO 80322.

An excellent pamphlet on car safety for babies, *Safe Passage,* is available from Questor, 1801 Commerce St., Piqua, OH 45356. Send a long, self-addressed stamped envelope.

No One Said
It Would Be Easy

If my children fuss when I strap them in, I tell them I'm doing it because I love them.

Doreen Newell, Simpsonville, SC

My 1-year-old loves rock 'n' roll, so I turn on the car radio and she has a blast as long as she likes the song. Otherwise, to keep her happy, we stick to short drives.

Cynthia Gillian, Texas City, TX

We've tried everything! When all else fails, *sing*! Never once has our singing failed to calm our daughter. We do get hoarse on long trips, though!

Paul and Leisa Thigpen, Julian, CA

My boys fussed when they were infants, but I never gave in and took them out. I guess I was most influenced when a Mercedes rear-ended my VW Beetle when my oldest was 3 months old. He was hardly shaken up.

Kathy Hickok, Delray Beach, FL

Up until about the age of 2, my son Chris (now 3) would cry and/or scream whenever he was in his car seat. *Nothing* amused him! Long trips were out of the question. Short fifteen-minute jaunts were long enough! Now our misery has finally paid off. Chris climbs into his car seat happily and even reminds us to buckle up.

Linda Newberry, Jermyn, PA

Car Seat Blues

When your baby is awake and behaving well in a car restraint, a little positive reinforcement can go a long way toward keeping the peace. Talk and play with your baby to make riding in a car fun. Frequent praise and attention can teach your child that travel in a car restraint is a positive experience. Decorate the seat and personalize it for your baby to make it special. If your baby is in a rear-facing car seat, tape a brightly-colored picture to the seat of the car for visual stimulation. Or attach a soft overhead mobile to the car seat. Do remember, though, that nothing keeps little ones entertained for very long, so be sure to stop frequently on long trips to let them stretch and get some fresh air.

One of the best ways to prevent discipline problems is to keep the children happily occupied. If you're prepared with toys and activities, the trip will be more pleasant for everyone. Start a series of silly rules, such as hands up to hold up a bridge when you go under one, or holding your breath when you go by a cemetery, or no talking when crossing a bridge. Silly word games, from making up crazy menus to calling things by their wrong names, can fill a car with laughter and fun.

What if, in spite of all your good intentions and best efforts, your properly restrained baby begins to scream as you drive down the interstate? Or your toddler chooses this time to throw a full-scale tantrum? Ideally, you'd pull off the highway to save the driver from dangerous distraction and to soothe the child, but it's not always possible to do that at the exact moment you'd like to. If you can't stop, try distracting the child:

- Turn up the radio, play a tape, or sing a loud song. Babies aren't particular about your choice of tunes. They just enjoy the sound of your voice!

- Rub the baby's chest gently and talk in soft, soothing tones.

- Try talking gently into the baby's palm, or put his or her hand on your throat. The vibration the baby feels from your vocal cords may have a soothing effect.

- Bring out a new toy or a snack.

- Tell children of 2 or 3 that if things get out of hand, you will pull the car off the road and stay there until they behave. It is wonderfully effective!

Short Car Trips

Once you leave home in a car, it becomes a trip, no matter how far you go—be it to the store, a restaurant, or the other side of town. If you're planning a longer car trip, it's a good idea to take your child on a lot of errands and such to help him or her get used to riding.

Be Prepared

- Keep an emergency disposable diaper in your glove compartment or trunk. Include other extras, such as Band-Aids, that might come in handy.

- Add a pacifier to your key chain, in case your child has emergency use for one.

- Store an extra set of diaper pins on your key chain to use when tape-tabs lose their stick or for attaching a napkin as an instant bib, or for any quick repairs.

- Carry a stretch belt in your purse to use as a "safety belt" for a toddler in a grocery cart, shopping center stroller, or restaurant high chair.

- Keep a treat hidden in your handbag to tide you over when needed. If the treat is noticed before you leave, it will probably be consumed immediately upon departure.

- Invest in a used stroller to keep in the trunk for those times you didn't plan to get out of the car, but do. A second car seat is also a good secondhand purchase if you have two cars. Be sure the seat was made after January 1981; if it was, it must conform to certain safety regulations. The manufacturer can confirm that for you and supply any missing or damaged parts you may need to replace. You can send a self-addressed business-size stamped envelope to the National Child Passenger Safety Association, P.O. Box 841, Ardmore, PA 19003 if you need instructions for an older car seat. Include manufacturer's name and model number.

Lost and Found "Insurance"

New places are enticing to toddlers, and they're often tempted to wander away and explore. The solution to a child's getting lost is, of course, prevention.

- Bring along a child's harness if your toddler is very active and tends to wander. The harness may look "bad" to purists, but it can be a real lifesaver. To modify its look, decorate with ribbon trim or embroidery.
- Have your child wear an identification tag or bracelet.
- Dress two or more ambulatory youngsters in matching T-shirts so they will be easier to spot in a crowd. In the winter, red hats are helpful.
- Create a special "family whistle" that children will recognize if they become lost or separated in a crowd, and practice using it at home.
- Point out police officers or guards to children so they will know whom to ask for help if they get lost. This can be especially useful abroad, where children aren't familiar with the different uniforms.

Shopping Center Trips

- Place your infant seat in the shopping center stroller for easy mobility.

- Shop early before stores get crowded so you don't get stuck in a long check-out line with an infant who suddenly needs to be fed.

- Tie toys to strollers with short strings to avoid the "I throw, you pick up" game.
- Attach a helium balloon to a stroller to intrigue and occupy a child—for a while.
- Bring a large shopping bag to hold hats, mittens, and snowsuits, and attach it to the stroller handle with a chain of two or three safety pins.
- Bring along your backpack to hold purchases so your hands will be free.
- Remember that many department stores have food departments where you can buy a slice of cheese or a piece of fruit to appease a cranky child.

Long Car Trips

Some children travel well; others simply don't. A set of parents I know traveled extensively with their first and second children. They left for a year in Israel when the second was only 3 months old. But they opted to stay put for three years when their third child turned out to be a *very* bad traveler. I had to respect their decision because of their experience.

Other parents decide that long trips are simply not worth the hassle and tell their families that if they wish to see the baby, their house is open to them. Mental health for babies and parents can be an important ingredient for keeping all family ties intact! It is fair to classify a three-hour trip to Grandma and Grandpa's as a long car trip, not a short one. Don't fool yourself into thinking that any one-day outing will be without stress.

Remember that your travel objective is to get there safely and happily. If your objective is to get there *soon,* you might be foregoing "safely," and you will surely forego "happily."

AAA (American Automobile Association)

Membership entitles you to free maps, tour books, TripTik maps, route-planning assistance, travel agent services, American Express travelers cheques, and discounts on car rentals and other goods and services. For the toll-free number of the state office nearest you, call (800) 555-1212.

Packing the Car

- Pack cereal, formula, small jars of baby food, extra bottles, and cleanup gear in a sturdy box that can be reached easily while you're on the road and carried in when you stop for the night. You may also want to include a bottle warmer or baby-food grinder.

- Make tissues, disposable wipes, and paper towels standard equipment in your car.

- Make a slipcover for the front seat with pockets that hang over the back to hold books, games, and toys. Or use a large cloth bag with a strap that fits over the head rest of the front seat.

- Store children's clothes or bulky cold-weather items in a duffel bag. It will fit easily into the car or trunk and can double as a pillow. Or get duffel bags for all, for the same reasons.

- Pack bulky items in a laundry basket if you have room for it in the car. At your destination use it for dirty clothes, so that when you get home, the basket and its contents can go straight to the laundry room.

- Pack children's clothes in different-colored pillow cases for easy identification.

- Keep a blanket or two handy during the winter in case your child gets cold, or in case you have car trouble and have to wait for help in the cold.

> Our 2-year-old loves to "pack" for long car rides. She has her own large plastic mesh shopping bag and fills it with her choice of toys and books.
> *Maureen Wilkins, Ketchum, ID*

- Carry one large plastic garbage bag for each day you plan to be in the car. This doesn't guarantee that the car will stay clean, but it will be a big help for nightly cleanups. Extras come in handy for dirty laundry. **(Remember, these can be dangerous and should not be used for play by small children.)**

- Consider investing in (or renting) a rooftop carrier to allow the inside of the car to be less cramped.

- Don't try to take *everything* to Grandma's. For example, a folding umbrella stroller and a small folding playpen that can double as a crib should serve most of your needs without taking up all your trunk space.

> For long trips, I make sure the children are dry, comfortably dressed, well fed, and approaching naptime before setting out. Then they usually fall peacefully asleep and we're all happy.
> *Helen Parljuk, Hastings, MN*

Motion Sickness

Car sickness used to be a common problem for small children, but parents aren't talking about it much anymore. Increased use of car seats, lower highway speeds, and smoother-riding cars may be the reasons.

If your child *is* bothered by car sickness, there are precautions you can take:

- Keep your child on a high-carbohydrate, low-fat diet for a few days before the trip. Go easy on liquids—especially milk and soft drinks—just before you leave.
- Have the child sit in the front seat, if the car restraint will fit there, so he or she can look *forward* out the window.
- Direct your child's attention to things outside the car in the distance, rather than at the side of the road. Don't let the child do close work such as looking at books or coloring.
- Open a window to let in fresh air, and don't smoke.
- Believe it or not, static electricity can cause nausea. If it's a problem, attach a wire or small chain to the rear axle so that it just touches the road.
- Offer Dramamine® as a preventative measure for children 2 years or older.
- If nausea is severe, stop the car and have the child recline with eyes closed and head motionless.

Rest Stops

If you treat stops as interesting experiences rather than delays, everyone will have a much better time.

There's no need to stop at a scheduled time if everyone is happily occupied or napping, but about every two hours take a break so everyone can stretch and so mobile children can run and burn up some energy. The best rest stop is one that offers both a stretch and food—*think picnic*. If you haven't brought the fixin's with you, you can stop at a store and pick up everything you need. Many towns have centrally located park areas; ask about them. Or just stop when you see some picnic tables, and break out a special snack you've been saving.

- When you stop, park in the shade, or cover the children's car seats with blankets to prevent them from becoming "hot seats."

- Let everyone know that you are planning to stop, so the kids will have something to look forward to and so older children will have time to put toys away and put on shoes.

- Be sure toddlers use the bathroom before you leave so you don't have to stop five minutes later.

The number of potty stops and diaper changes will always be in direct proportion to the amount of liquid consumed in transit!

It Worked for Us

We carefully plan routes that go by state parks when we take long trips. That way we have nice places to stop and eat and play with the girls. It's much nicer than feeding a baby on the side of the road with cars whizzing by. The scenery is nicer on back roads, too.

G. Moore, Houston, TX

At gas stops, everybody, including toddlers, gets out and exercises, and then changes places in the car (move that car seat, too, to give that sitter a different traveling partner and view). At the picnic stops, we've had our older ones do ten laps around the picnic tables!

Anita Holland, Minnetonka, MN

When my children were small, we always brought a large empty coffee can with a lid to use as a portable toilet or barf bag. (Yes, we used it!)

Sidney Milstone, Lathrup Village, MI

I point out trucks to my son and he talks nonstop about their color, size, contents, etc. I make sure his car seat is raised high enough so he has a clear view out of his window. My 1-year-old is afraid of traveling at night, so I place his car seat beside me up front and open the glove compartment. It has a small light inside that serves as a night light for him.

Janet Stabile, Ellington, CT

My son hated being in the seat at night. We got him a small flashlight after I finally figured out that car and street lights were scaring him.

Michal Doesburg, Orange, CA

6

Going by Airplane, Train, or Bus

If you don't travel by car, your destination, your budget, and your personal inclinations will help you choose among three alternatives: the airplane, the train, and the bus. Flying is the fastest, a real blessing for long-distance travel with babies or toddlers. Despite lack of space for babies and baggage, and possible delays and discomfort from changes in cabin pressure, it's the easiest way to go.

Train travel offers the advantages of the passing scenery and a bit more freedom of movement, but it has its disadvantages, too. Riding the bus is probably your last choice—but it costs the least, and it will get you to corners of the country where planes and trains simply don't go.

Flying

The noise of a plane, even more than that of a car, helps lull a newborn infant to sleep. The more awake and aware toddler requires full-time entertainment from the parent. Obviously, the shorter the trip, the easier the job.

If you have a choice, make the time zones work with you rather than against you. North–south travel will always be less disruptive than east–west travel. But any trip causing more than a two-hour time adjustment will take just that—adjustment.

Take heart if all does *not* go smoothly. If your child travels regularly by air from infancy, by the time he or she is 3 or 4 years old the child will be a seasoned traveler who will be delighted with toilets that flush blue water and with overhead lights he or she can control.

Making Reservations

If you are pregnant, inquire about airline policies. Some airlines have restrictions against accepting passengers during the late stages of their pregnancy.

Children 2 and under fly free in the United States and for 10 percent of adult fare on international flights. The child will not be assigned a seat; you can hope for an empty one to use. Otherwise, your child will sit on your lap during the flight as well as for takeoffs and landings. If you're flying alone internationally with two children under 2 years of age, you will have to pay half fare for one of the children, but you will also have a reserved seat for one child.

Many domestic carriers offer reduced fares for children over 2, but ages and offers vary. Airline deregulation has led to a reduction in family fares in general, so it is best to consult

> My daughter was 4 but petite. Since air travel was so expensive, I decided to try to get her on as 2 by holding her and covering her with a blanket. Certainly it was worth a try. I was standing in line in front of the travel agent confirming my seat reservation when the person behind me, apparently taken by my daughter, asked her how old she was. In a loud voice she replied, "I'm 4, but my mother said to say I'm 2."
>
> *Hallie Lerman, Los Angeles, CA*

a travel agent, who can arrange, by computer, the most economical flight for your family.

Inquire whether a meal will be served. Some airlines offer special children's meals; request them when making reservations, or at least twenty-four hours before takeoff. Keep in mind that all airline food is prepared by flight kitchens on the ground ahead of time. If you have a fussy eater, bring your own meal or snack.

Although some airlines will make reserved seating arrangements by phone, most will not, unless you're traveling first class on a business flight, or, sometimes, if you've reserved a bassinet. However, this system is changing rapidly, and it is best to confirm details with the airline directly.

- Reserve a bassinet ahead of time if you need one. They're usually free, but the supply may be limited. Be aware that most are only 27 inches long and 12½ inches wide, so if your baby is bigger than that or weighs more than 30 pounds, you won't be able to use one. Sometimes bassinets go on the floor, and sometimes they attach to

On a family vacation, we had a short stopover at the Los Angeles airport. As we waited for our plane, trying to keep tabs on two active children, we suddenly heard the ear-shattering blast of the airport alarm siren. I dived under the nearest chair, fearing we'd be blown up any minute. I looked frantically for my husband and children, and finally saw my son standing behind a NO ADMITTANCE sign with his hand on a switch and a "now what do I do?" expression on his face. I walked quickly to the ladies' room and remained there until our plane was called, letting Father handle the situation.

Gail Dodge, Wilmington, NC

the bulkhead seat. Find out which is the case for your flight. If the bassinet attaches to the bulkhead seat, you may wish to reserve one simply to get that often-favored seat. Keep in mind that the bassinet will not assure safety in turbulence.

- Select flight times that don't coincide with feeding times, say some travelers, although you'll be nursing or bottle-feeding an infant during takeoff and landing to reduce ear discomfort from changes in air pressure. Others say it's more important to avoid flight times that coincide with naptime.

- Try to avoid peak travel hours in the morning or early evening, when the plane is likely to be full. Putting up with the inconvenience of even a late-night flight may mean that there will be an extra seat for your child, as well as the possibility of more help from airline attendants.

- Ask for a flight that originates in your city (if possible) to ensure better seat selection.

- Choose a nonstop flight when you can, so you won't have to deal with extra landings and takeoffs that cause air pressure changes and the hassles of changing planes and waiting in airline terminals. (Alternatively, choose flights that offer extra time between flights rather than cutting it close. That extra airport stopover time gives a mobile child the chance to run and stretch, which fortunately is acceptable airport behavior.)

Choosing the Best Seats

- Request the window and aisle seats in a three-seat row if you're traveling with one child (under 2) and another adult, and hope that the middle seat won't be taken. If it is, the occupant will probably be happy to exchange seats so that your family can sit together . . . with your child now on your lap.

- Consider asking for the window seat if you are alone and traveling with an infant. A window seat also offers the most privacy for breast-feeding. Choose the aisle seat if you are alone with a mobile toddler so you won't constantly have to climb over passengers for a trip to the bathroom or some aisle-sightseeing.

- Ask for seats on the same side of the aisle if you're traveling with two adults and more than one child. Tending children who are in front of or behind you will be easier than reaching across the aisle, which will be impossible while attendants serve food or drinks. Flight rules require one adult per child in a row, in case it's necessary to handle oxygen masks.

- Choose seats away from busy areas such as the galley if you are hoping your child will take a nap.

- Ask for seats at least several rows in front of the smoking section if you are not picking the bulkhead seats.

- Be sure the bulkhead seats you get on a jumbo jet are on the center aisle, not by the doors. Small children are not allowed to occupy seats next to these emergency doors, so you'll be required to move if you were inadvertently assigned these seats. (But also be aware that some airlines have a limited number of oxygen masks available in the bulkhead area and might not be able to seat families there.)

Pros and Cons of
Bulkhead Seats

Many parents feel that seats in the bulkhead are best for traveling with small children. These seats face the walls that separate the different sections of the cabin. They allow room for you to stretch your legs, arrange the children's paraphernalia, or change a nonmessy diaper on the floor. A child can't annoy a passenger in front of you—only behind you!

One disadvantage is that the position of meal trays in the bulkhead may make it difficult for you to tend a child as you eat. Also, there is no storage room under the seat, so the attendant will move your carry-on baggage out of your reach during takeoff and landing.

If you're traveling on a jumbo jet, the bulkhead seats in the center aisle will be near the lavatories, which means that there may be a line of waiting passengers hovering about you in the aisles. On the bright side, these people may help entertain your child.

Other parents prefer seats near the rear of the plane. You'll be close to the flight attendants, whose assistance you may need and whose activities may amuse the children.

Using Your Car Seat on the Airplane

Car seats approved by the FAA (Federal Aviation Administration) can now be used during takeoff and landing, if you have reserved and paid for the child's seat, regardless of age. If you have not paid for a seat for your child under the age of 2, you can use the car seat if an extra seat is available. If you have brought the car seat on board and there is no extra seat, the flight attendant may stow for you or, more likely, check it as baggage.

Although it's not mandatory, the FAA recommends using the approved car seat in a window seat for the convenience of the other passengers. It *can't* be used in the emergency exit access rows or in the rows just in front of and in back of them. The car seat must be properly secured to the passenger seat at all times during the flight, even when your child is not sitting in it.

When you board, the FMVSS label (Federal Motor Vehicle Safety Standard) should be attached to the seat, indicating make and model number. Many car restraints (most models by Cosco/Peterson, Century, Strolee, and Pride-Trimble) have now been approved, but it is wise to check the airline's policies to be sure they will accept a seat with an FMVSS label and whether they will require purchase of a ticket for the car seat's use.

To find out if your car seat has been approved for use, call the FAA at (202) 426-8374 weekdays between 8:30 A.M. and 4:30 P.M. EST.

Flight Preparations

- Arrive at the airport at least fifteen minutes earlier than if you were traveling alone. You'll need the extra time when you have children along.

- Confirm your seat reservations, if you made them ahead of time, as soon as you arrive. Don't assume the computer is flawless!

- Explain to your toddler that all items, even favorite teddies, must be given up for a moment to pass through the security check, but that they will be returned in just a minute.

- Attach a luggage or ID tag to your toddler. Include name, destination, etc. Remember to list allergies or medical needs on the tag. At the very least, write your child's name and the address and phone number of your destination on a piece of paper and pin it to his or her clothing if you will be in any place where there is a chance for wandering. (Some people feel it is safer to list business addresses on luggage.)

- In your carry-on luggage, include *everything* you'll need in case your other luggage is lost. Consider putting the contents of your purse into a heavy-duty resealable plastic bag that fits into the flight bag, eliminating one more item to carry.

- Pack your flight/baby bag with one whole day's worth of supplies and clothing for the children. (There is nothing worse than being stranded in soiled clothes, or without enough diapers or formula.)

- Consider taking along a coverall or apron to protect *you*. That way you don't have to worry about a change of clothes for yourself.

Before You Board

- Look for specific areas designated as nurseries, now available in many large airports. These are unattended areas near ladies' rooms, with extra space, seating, and a variety of amenities. Some European airport nurseries are supervised, so you can leave your child while you check in.

- Double-diaper your baby before boarding; diaper-changing space on a plane is basically nonexistent. If you must make a change on board, use your seat space only if your family is occupying three contiguous seats, or use the floor if you have the bulkhead seats. Otherwise you will have to use the toilet lid in the bathroom—not easy, but possible. Bring a towel or small piece of folded, washable vinyl to put under the baby for diaper changing.

- Consider bringing your own brown-bag meal. Even though children over 2 are entitled to a meal, that doesn't mean they'll eat it, or that it will come when your child is hungry.

- Bring a lightweight baby blanket with you. It can be used to form a makeshift tent to help cut off visual stimulation if you are trying to get your baby to sleep.

On airplane trips, an umbrella stroller is wonderful. In the bulkhead seat, we can set it up, put the child in it, and have some free hands.
Becky Gammons, Beaverton, OR

- Check your baby's car restraint with your luggage if you are not going to use it in flight. Be sure to tag it with your name and address. Packing it in a large, heavy-duty plastic garbage bag, while not required, will help protect it.

- Forewarn a child who's old enough to understand that running in the aisles is not allowed and that "playground voices" aren't, either.

- Let your toddler carry his or her own little flight bag or wear a small backpack with special toys or snacks inside.

On Board

- Take advantage of the system that allows parents with small children to board before everyone else. This gives you time to get settled. With a restless toddler, however, you might wish to board last.

- Help yourself to pillows and a blanket from the overhead luggage rack before takeoff, as there probably will not be enough for each passenger if the flight is full.

- Carry an infant in a soft front pack to free your hands. Make sure the seat belt is over *your* pelvis and not the baby's during takeoff and landing.

- Remove the armrest between seats (except in the bulkhead, where it's not removable) to give a child room to stretch out. The flight attendant can help you.

- Put a big bib on your toddler and remove it just before you land if you want to arrive with a clean child.

- Don't forget to ask the airline attendant for in-flight mementos such as a wing pin, a deck of cards, or a postcard. Ask for these items shortly after takeoff. When the flight attendants get busy, they may not have time to bring them right away.

- Be sure there are airsick bags in your seat pockets. You can use the bags for soiled diapers, too, but be sure to give them to the flight attendant to dispose of properly. Do not leave them in seat pockets when you disembark!

- Be prepared for unusual behavior from your child. The child who *always* naps may fool you, and your gregarious baby may cry when a stranger acts friendly.

Coping with Cabin Pressure Changes

Most ear problems in the air occur when a plane is changing altitudes, especially when it's descending. Smaller children are more susceptible to discomfort, as the eustachian tubes in their ears are narrower and more prone to collapse with altitude changes.

- Let your baby nurse or suck on a bottle or pacifier during takeoff and landing to reduce pressure on ears. A hungry child will suck more vigorously, so don't feed your baby just before you take off. Babies' sucking reflex can be activated by touching their lips, or having them suck on your finger.

- Give gum or lollipops to older children during takeoff and landing.

- Try to get your child to yawn, which helps make ears "pop" and relieves pressure, as do other exaggerated facial movements. Make a game of making faces.

- Or hold a child's nose closed while he or she swallows to "pop" ears open. Several swallows may be necessary.

- Ask the flight attendant for help if air pressure changes cause ear pain for your child. The attendant can provide two cups containing hot, moist towels to be held over the ears to reduce discomfort.

- If your child has a cold and must fly, ask your doctor to recommend or prescribe an oral decongestant. And be sure the child sits upright during descent.

- Be aware that clogged or painful ears can take as long as three days to return to normal. If your child has problems after that, see a doctor.

In-Flight Nourishment

Remember the old Scout creed "Be prepared" and don't travel without formula for a bottle-fed baby and snacks for older youngsters.

- Ask the flight attendant for water or juice for yourself and your toddler, before takeoff or later on. Dry air in the plane can cause a sore or scratchy throat and a dry nose, especially on very long flights. Bring liquids for your baby. Don't expect that you will get service just when you need it.

- Ask also about the best time to get help with warming the baby's food or bottle, if warming is important to you. (Babies usually don't care.)

- The free cola drinks airlines offer contain caffeine, which can "speed up" kids and keep them from sleeping, as well as keep you running to the bathroom with them.

WARNING
Don't drink any hot beverage when flying
with a small child. A spilled drink
can burn a child—or you!

Those L-o-n-g Flights

- Let an active toddler jog around the airport to tire himself or herself out before boarding the plane.

- Remember that airport gift shops sell a good selection of last-minute games and toys. Look for quiet games designed for travel, but be wary of small pieces that can be lost or swallowed.

- Gift wrap some small toys or favorite munchies and hand them out, one at a time, as a reward for a toddler's good behavior. Pass out these surprises every half hour or so (depending on the length of the flight), but only on the condition that the child continues to play quietly.

- Ask the flight attendant for feminine napkin pads to use inside a disposable or cloth diaper to stretch your diaper supply if you think you are running short.

- Help children space games and activities to prevent boredom.

- Don't expect a young child to be entertained for long by in-flight movies or music. Bring a cassette player of your own in case the airline's selection of entertainment doesn't interest your child. The headsets the airlines provide are not always comfortable on the ears. (Remember that radio headsets can't be used because they interfere with the plane's radio transmissions.) If your cassette player can record, all the better; its entertainment value will be expanded.

Anticipating Jet Lag

For some reason that is not well understood, it is easier for people to adjust to a flight going west rather than east. The more time zones you cross, the longer it will take your child to adjust.

- Try to have everyone well rested before starting out.

- Changing time zones also affects eating schedules. Try demand-feeding your baby for a while until he or she adjusts. Eating schedules will adjust sooner than sleep routines.

- To minimize adjustment periods, pick flights that depart as early in the day as possible when flying east, and as late as is realistic when flying west.

- Allow for recovery time when you get to where you are going, but try to adjust to the clock on the wall from the start.

Keeping our child entertained was our biggest problem. For long car or plane trips with a 1- to 2-year-old, fill an old wallet with expired credit cards, or heavy paper cut to the same size and some cards from an old deck of cards. Our daughter spent several minutes looking at each before throwing it down. Also fill containers with small objects such as shells, small toys, and so on. Picture books and *National Geographic* kept her attention for long stretches, too.

Barbara Deleebeeck, Stavanger, Norway

My two-year-old and I were flying to see my parents. He had been playing quietly with his dozen or so Matchbox cars. The plane began its descent gently but not gently enough to keep those little cars on the tray. Over the top they went, to roll under twelve rows of seats ahead of us. I spent the time before we were ordered to buckle up for landing canvassing the aisle. "Pardon me, sir, but if you look under your seat I think you'll find . . ."

Phyllis Anderson, Los Angeles, CA

With kids 2 and under, be prepared for everything you can think of and then realize that the one thing you haven't thought of will happen. Expect to be embarrassed and, if you hear people mentioning you to their friends in the baggage claim area ("There's the lady with the baby who screamed for forty-five minutes"), take some comfort from the fact that you're not the only one to whom this has happened and that you'll never see these people again!

Sharon Amastae, El Paso, TX

Deplaning

• Accept any help offered.

• Take the unused airsick bag with you for future cleanup needs.

• Don't feel you have to be first off the plane when you land. Use your judgment. Standing in a hot, crowded aisle with a child or two can ruin your arrival.

- Make a potty stop once off the plane and on your way to the baggage claim area. The stalls for the handicapped usually are roomy enough to allow you to bring your child, seated in a stroller, in with you.

- Mark your luggage with distinctive ribbons or stickers so your child can help you spot it quickly as it comes down the conveyor belt.

Train Travel

Train travel often offers spectacular views of the countryside, usually of more interest to adults than to small children. It also allows more freedom of movement than either air or car travel, although if you're on a long trip, you'll find sleeping accommodations cramped. Although it can be pleasant for adults, don't delude yourself: a long train trip with an active toddler can be very wearing.

Reserving Your Space

Train travel is relatively inexpensive. Amtrak offers family fares that make it even more attractive.

head of household	full fare
spouse	50% fare
children 12 to 21	50% fare
children 2 to 11	25% fare
children under 2	free

Reservation procedures vary depending on where you're going. On some long-distance routes you can reserve a private compartment for your family. This is an added expense, of course, and you'll have to decide if it's worth it. For the specifics of your particular route, brochures, and timetables, call or write:

Amtrak Distribution Center
P.O. Box 7717
Itasca, IL 60143
800-USA-RAIL

- Consider taking a night train to get you where you're going while the family sleeps.

- Get to the depot early if you haven't reserved a compartment. Your reservations will not be for specific seats, and you'll want to be able to find seats together.

- Try to get seats directly in a row. Many seats face each other.

- Check whether a dining car will be available. Most are only on long-distance trains. Snack-bar service is available on shorter trips. Consider bringing your own snacks and sandwiches to save money and to be sure the food will appeal to your child.

Other Considerations

- Choose a nonsmoking car for your child's comfort. Take a break in a smoking car if you smoke and can leave your child in the charge of a responsible adult.

- Request pillows and blankets; temperatures in trains vary. If you are only on a day trip these might not be available, so consider bringing your own.

- Bring all baby-care items you need with you. You won't be able to buy them on the train.

- Plan to bring no more luggage than you can handle by yourself. Porters aren't always available. If you do need special assistance, ask the conductor to call ahead for a porter to meet you at the platform. Some Amtrak stations have free luggage carts, but you can't always count on their availability at busy times.

- Take a narrow umbrella stroller so you can walk your baby up and down the aisle.

- Wedge a backpack with a metal frame or stand on a seat to let a child see out the window, or bring your car restraint. Either can be used as a booster seat in the dining car.

- Watch your mobile toddler closely. Playing or running in the aisles is annoying to others—and dangerous. Encourage cautious walking, as rough places in the tracks can throw anyone off balance easily.

- Warm food or formula by putting the container into running hot water in a bathroom basin. Or ask food-service people to warm bottles and baby food for you.

- Remember that each passenger car will have a water dispenser.

Bus Travel

Bus travel is the least expensive kind of public transportation, but it's also the most difficult with very young children. Cramped quarters, frequent stops, and a stuffy atmosphere make buses less appealing for everyone concerned, especially on long trips.

- Be prepared to hold your baby on your lap for the entire ride. There are no other accommodations for infants, unless you purchase a second seat.

- Practice changing your baby in your lap. The bathroom on a bus is too small for it.

- Bring everything you'll need for the baby in a small bag that's easy to handle. If the bus is crowded, you won't have much room for carry-on luggage.

- Try to get the seats at the front of the bus where your child will be able to see out the windows more easily.

- Pack a transistor radio with headphones to entertain your child. Reception is especially good near the windows.

- Take food, at least for the children. Meal stops are limited in time and not always at places you would choose.

- Carry your own motion-sickness bag, just in case. Buses don't provide them.

7

Traveling Abroad

❦

Traveling abroad with an infant or a small child can be an exciting adventure. The universal appeal of a baby can enhance your trip as much as it complicates it, and many parents have found that their *bambino* has provided an entree for warm experiences. What you lose in romantic evenings you may make up in friendly encounters.

If your budget allows, you may want to consider an *au pair* girl (usually a student) who will travel with you, help with your child or children, be generally useful, and who can even act as an interpreter and guide. There are employment agencies that specialize in placing *au pairs*. European newspapers have ads placed by such young women looking for this type of work.

Flexibility is again the key. A rested and well-fed child (not to mention parent) is vital to the success of extended travel. Don't get into the trap of "getting your money's worth." When your child needs rest, stop and get yours, too.

Getting Ready to Go

Try to plan for a stay of three to four days in any one place to create a minimum of upheaval in your child's routine. And give yourself at least one day a week without any activity scheduled, just to catch up.

Planes on transoceanic flights will carry baby supplies if the airline knows there will be a baby on board, so let them know. These are really meant for emergency use when you run short. Bring what you need with you.

Don't expect anyone else to provide anything for your baby, and you won't be disappointed. Plan ahead, make lists of what you'll need, pack accordingly, and your trip should go smoothly.

Passports and Visas

All U.S. citizens, including infants, must have passports to visit foreign countries (except Canada, Mexico, and some Caribbean islands). Applications for passports are accepted at your local courthouse or at a U.S. Passport Agency office. Passports are valid for 5 years for children under 18, and for 10 years for adults. First passports cost $27 for children under 18, and $42 for adults. Renewal rates are lower.

A few countries also require visas. A visa is the official stamp in your passport that allows you to enter a specific foreign country. First, find out if the country you'll be visiting requires one. If it does, apply to the consulate of the country you wish to visit, sending along your passport and a photo. It's usually a relatively simple matter, but it may be more complicated if you are planning a trip to Eastern Europe. Your best bet is to consult a travel agent who is familiar with making these arrangements.

- Make your travel plans early. A passport can take six weeks or longer to process, especially during peak travel times (spring and summer), when many others are applying. It may take a month or more to obtain visas from each country you plan to visit. However, if you *are* rushed, make the fact known; special arrangements may be possible.

- You can apply for a passport for a child under 13 without having the child present.

- Take certified copies of birth certificates (with a *raised* stamp imprint) for each family member when applying for passports. Adults will also need a driver's license or other picture identification. Call ahead to see if you'll need anything else.

- Arrange for a passport photographer (look in the Yellow Pages) to take the photographs you will need. Be sure to find out how many copies you'll need. Visas require pictures, too. Call ahead and allow sufficient time for processing. If you don't go to a photographer who specializes in passport photos, be sure you know what rules apply before you have your picture taken by someone else.

- Carry several extra passport photos with you in case you lose your passport or change plans on the journey and need visas for countries not listed in your passport. Keep a record of your passport number and the place and date of its issue in your wallet. If you lose your passport, report this to a U.S. embassy or consulate.

- Photocopy every health record and vital document you might possibly need.

Car Rentals Abroad

- Keep in mind that car labels such as "intermediate size" don't necessarily mean the same abroad as they do here.

- Have any reservation confirmed in writing. (This applies to hotels as well.) Ask which credit cards they accept.

- Bring your infant car seat if you'll be traveling by car. Be sure it's an FAA-approved model so you can also use it on the airplane. (See page 80.) Many foreign car-rental agencies don't have them, and the ones that do often will not allow you to make one-way rentals. Avis, Hertz, Budget, and National have car seat rentals available in some cities. Check when you make your overseas car-rental reservations.

Other Overseas Auto Rentals

Auto Europe
P.O. Box 500
Yorktown Heights, NY 10598
(800) 223-5555

Europe Car Hire
P.O. Box 7402
Ventura, CA 93006
(805) 644-2323

Essentials

- Leave a detailed itinerary with friends or relatives so you can be reached in an emergency. Give them your passport number and insurance information, too.

- Confirm international flights seventy-two hours before departure.

Diaper Metrics

Know your baby's weight in kilos if you want to buy the right size. Disposable-diaper sizes are determined by weight, which in most countries is measured in kilos, not pounds.

1 KILO   = 2.2 POUNDS
10 KILOS = 22 POUNDS

- Pack plenty of disposable diapers—perhaps an entire duffel bag or soft-sided suitcase full—unless you're prepared to make do with whatever you can get. Although some American brands of disposables are available abroad, you may not be able to find them at your location. European disposables are more expensive, and some are simply thick cotton pads designed to fit into rubber pants. The quality of different types varies, so be prepared to experiment.

- Bring children's clothes that can be washed in a hotel sink and drip-dried overnight. As in this country, laundromats are available too, and many places will also fold your laundry. Drop off dirty laundry in the morning and pick it up later that day or the next morning.

- Pack lightweight clothing that can be layered—both for temperature control and laundry control.

- Don't forget your own mild soap and a washcloth; not all places provide them. Also carry along a good supply of small sample-size toiletries. You won't find them abroad.

- Pack a mild soap such as Ivory to help prevent diaper rash or irritation from harsh soaps used to launder clothes.

- Bring a soft-carrier, frame backpack or a collapsible stroller for sightseeing. These items can be carried aboard the plane. But in some countries (including ours), strollers will not always be allowed in public places such as museums and stores.

- Take a roll of soft toilet paper with the center core removed (so it takes up less room) for a multitude of uses, from cleaning bottoms to wiping runny noses.

In England many hotels offer something called "baby listening." There are intercoms in all the rooms, and if you request it, while you are in the dining room, at the pool, or elsewhere, someone will listen for your child to awaken, and notify you. When this service is not available, you can take the phone off the hook and the operator will listen for the baby.

Mary McNamara, Wayzata, MN

Medical Matters

Immunizations are *not* required for travel to Europe, the Soviet Union, Japan, and many other countries. However, if you will be visiting some South American, Asian, or central African countries, it's advisable to be vaccinated against cholera and yellow fever. It's also a good idea to check with your pediatrician to make sure the children are up to date on their regular immunizations.

If you have a choice, it is wise to wait until your child is at least 18 months old before you travel abroad. By then your child will have been immunized against the major childhood diseases, including polio, outbreaks of which have been reported recently in Central and South America. If a small child contracts a serious disease (malaria, for instance), it is much harder to treat given the choice of medicines available for use with a small child. Breast-feeding a baby doesn't protect against these serious diseases.

Preventive inoculations or vaccinations for cholera and yellow fever are not recommended for infants under 6 months. Injections for typhoid can be given after 6 weeks of age but usually cause severe reactions. Protection against certain types of malaria can be given to any age baby. All of these need to be given at least 10 days before departure.

- Discuss with your pediatrician any medical problems your child may have that could cause difficulties while you're traveling. Ask for recommendations about diet, sunscreens, or medication for motion sickness. Your doctor may also be able to give you a list of physicians and medical facilities at your destination.

- Get the generic names of medications you may need to purchase abroad. Brand names will vary. You will find that many drugs available only by prescription here can be bought over the counter abroad.

- Remember to carry all prescription drugs in their original containers when traveling out of the country, or you may run into trouble at customs. Also bring copies of the prescriptions. Keep them in your carry-on luggage so you'll still have them if your other luggage is lost.

- Inquire at the American embassy or consulate if you want names of English-speaking physicians in that country. But keep in mind that since English tends to be the language most doctors are trained in, you probably will not have a problem being understood in most situations.

Two Medical Help Services

Intermedic, 777 Third Avenue, New York, NY 10017, offers yearly family memberships and provides access to doctors in 200 cities and 90 countries.

IAMAT (International Association for Medical Assistance to Travelers), 736 Center St., Lewiston, NY 14092, can give you names of English-speaking physicians, and locations of hospitals in 450 cities and 200 countries. Also available is information on climate, sanitation, and immunization laws.

Precautions Against the "Runs"

Stomach upsets abroad usually are caused by bacteria and organisms that are just *different* from the ones our bodies are used to. The problem usually occurs as a result of changes in water supplies and the use of different fertilizers from country to country, but it can occur from place to place within countries as well.

When traveling abroad, diarrhea is a real health concern. It is inconvenient at best, and it can be serious, especially in very young children, because it can lead to dehydration. This can be critical with a child under the age of 6 months, and it certainly needs to be watched carefully with a child under the age of 12 months. If your child has five or more watery bowel movements a day for three or more days in a row, get medical attention. If the diarrhea occurs in conjunction with other symptoms (fever, for example), consult a doctor as soon as possible.

Bring your own thermometer along if you are not good at converting Celsius to Fahrenheit.

- Be careful about drinking unchlorinated tap water in any country, and *do not* drink it in Latin America, Asia, or Africa. Remember that this warning applies to ice cubes and water used for brushing teeth. Most European cities have safe drinking water on tap. A good rule of thumb is always to drink bottled water in villages or rural areas.

- Don't let children swallow bath or shower water.

- Bring along a supply of water purification tablets. Or boil water for ten to fifteen minutes to purify it. A heating coil with the proper electrical adapter can be very useful for this purpose.

- Eat only foods that are cooked and peeled, if the quality of food is at all questionable.

- Bring powdered milk and/or formula (even if you are nursing—just in case) and mix it with bottled water only. It's a good idea to bring along enough ready-to-serve formula to hold your baby until you can find a reliable source of bottled water.

- Drink only milk and milk products that have been pasteurized. Boxed, unrefrigerated milk is common outside the United States and is safe to drink. It needs refrigeration only after opening, and it tastes like fresh milk.

- Bottled carbonated drinks are safe because the carbonation makes them too acidic for bacteria to survive.

- If drinking water is not chlorinated, odds are that the swimming pool will present the same problem.
- Check with a local American travel bureau to find restaurants known to prepare foods safe to eat. And keep in mind that most large hotels catering to American tourists are usually safe.

Dealing with Diarrhea

Even if it isn't serious, diarrhea can spoil your fun with diaper leaks, extra laundry, and bathroom-hopping. The best cure is to slow down, curtail activities, and give the body a chance to recover.

Over-the-counter drugs are not recommended for treating diarrhea in children. Defizzed 7-Up sometimes helps, and it's widely available. Cola drinks help too, but keep in mind that they contain caffeine.

Pepto-Bismol has proven effective for some, either taken daily as a preventive measure or to relieve symptoms when they occur, but it is not recommended for small children. Ask your pediatrician for a prescription medication before you go.

Home Remedy for a Run-of-the-Mill Case of the "Runs"

Mix one 3-ounce package of flavored gelatin with one cup of water and have your child drink as much as he or she can. The gelatin is a good binder, and the sweet taste encourages consumption.

- Replace lost fluids and electrolytes by drinking juices with a pinch of salt added, or tea made with safe boiled water with a bit of baking soda added.

- Encourage drinking of any safe liquids. Breast-fed babies should continue to be breast-fed.

- Eliminate solid food from the diet and switch to skim milk, or better yet, no milk, for a while. Ease back into a normal diet with bananas or toast, easily "portable" binding foods. Rice is always good and so is water that rice is cooked in.

Food for Thought

- Bring a hanging portable high chair (see page 50) for eating in restaurants, or be prepared to use your stroller, car seat, or lap. In Europe and Latin America especially, restaurants do not cater to babies. You'll find sidewalk cafes are more accommodating to children.

- Be prepared for the idiosyncrasies of foreign shopping. For example, in some countries powdered milk is available only in pharmacies, not in grocery stores.

- If you're breast-feeding, be aware that attitudes toward nursing in public are far more relaxed in most foreign countries than in the United States.

- Carry a box of instant baby cereal with you. It is very light in weight and you probably will not find your brand abroad.

- Availability of baby food and baby supplies varies widely from country to country. Before you leave, accustom your child to eating table foods puréed in a baby food grinder.

If your baby will eat only commercial baby food, bring your own emergency supply.

- Bring along a small can opener or Swiss Army knife. In some countries, you will find only canned baby food.

- Bring a good supply of peanut butter if your child is addicted to it. It's not as widely available in many countries as it is here.

Buying Infant Formula Abroad

If you don't pack your own infant formula, be aware that availability of familiar brands varies greatly from country to country. The three major American companies that make infant formula (Ross Laboratories, Mead Johnson, and Wyeth Labs) all distribute their products overseas, usually under the same product names. (One exception is Similac, which is sold as Multival in Germany.) The ingredients may vary slightly depending on local requirements. (Call a children's clinic, pediatrician, or pharmacist at your destination if you're concerned about this.) Most formula sold abroad is in the form of powder, which is less convenient, but more economical. Remember to mix the formula with bottled or boiled water only. The metric system won't pose a problem; just use the scoop provided as you normally would.

If you can't find the formula you want and you don't want to try what's available, call the American embassy and ask if you can shop in their store. Chances are they'll have your brand in liquid form.

- Bring packets of instant cocoa to mix with boiled water as one way to provide your child with calcium.

- Fast-food restaurants (other than a few American chains) are practically nonexistent in Europe. Children's menus are also rare. You can sometimes ask for a smaller portion for a child, for which you will usually pay less than full price.

- Plan to eat your main meal at noon. This is a tradition in many countries, anyway. Many restaurants don't welcome children at their evening meals, which are often long and leisurely and may begin very late.

- Always have more supplies (food or diapers) for your baby than you expect to need. One extra day's worth is often enough. And stock up before weekends, because store hours may be very limited.

Customs and Countries

Don't go with the attitude that only familiar American products will do for you and your child. Explore stores and try their wares. Some folks purposely "forget" items such as toothpaste so they can purchase local products that also are souvenirs to bring home. Think of your trip as educational and none of this will feel frustrating.

- Teach older children how to say simple phrases such as "please," "thank you," and "excuse me" in the language of the country you will be visiting. And keep a phrase book on hand at all times if you don't know the language. Picture "flash cards" are also available for communicating without words. If you need something and don't know the right word, you show someone a picture of it. It's primitive, but it works.

- Plan to make your own fun outdoors with your children in European parks. Playgrounds equipped with swings, seesaws, and such are very rare.

- Ask discreetly to use the men's or ladies' room, toilette, or WC (for water closet). Don't ask for the bathroom. It will be interpreted as your wanting a bath.

- Be prepared for public rest rooms that are not as clean or well equipped as the ones you're used to. You may be expected to pay for toilet paper, which often is of inferior quality. Carrying your own supply of individual tissue packages is a good solution.

- Carry disposable john-seat covers with you if you worry about hygiene in out-of-the-way places.

- Ask for special children's rates, which usually are available for transportation and sightseeing tours in Europe.

- Remember that while car rental in Europe may be convenient, a Eurailpass and a Eurail Youthpass (good in sixteen countries) are more economical. Children under age 4 will travel free. Children under age 12 pay half fare. You can sometimes buy them in Europe, but they're hard to come by and cost much more, so it's strongly recommended that you buy them before you leave home. Where reserved seats are required, this pass doesn't *guarantee* you a seat, so check into each train's requirements. Check with your travel agent or write to: Eurailpass, 610 Fifth Ave., Room 516, New York, NY 10020. For train travel in England, Scotland, and Wales, you will need a BritRail pass. Write to: BritRail, 630 Third Avenue, New York, NY 10017. If you will not be doing a lot of multi-country travel, even Eurail may not be your best bet. Ask your travel agent. And also ask about Eurotrain passes for children and students; these passes can be purchased only in Europe.

- Invest in a copy of *Fielding's Europe with Children* by Leila Hadley (New York: William Morrow, $12.95) for in-depth information on twenty European countries as well as general information on traveling with kids abroad.

Bon Voyage!